M000305527

kitchen
simplicity

TINY HOUSE FOODIE

kitchen simplicity
TINY HOUSE FOODIE

CARMEN SHENK

HD Media Press Inc.

First Edition

Paperback ISBN:

Library of Congress Control Number:

Published by HD Media Press Inc.
http://hdmediapress.com/
New York, NY

Cover & Design: Carmen Shenk

Produced in the United States of America

*to my beloved Austrian
who lives inside
a tiny house
but outside
conformity*

'Tis a gift to be simple

'Tis a gift to be free

'Tis the gift to come down

where we aught to be

And when we find ourselves

in the place just right

It will be in the valley

of love and delight.

-Joseph Brackett

chapter 1
liberation

I was a childless woman, and a Mennonite wife. And I had a secret: my marriage was over and my home had become a war zone. But staying married is what good Christian women do. Things finally deteriorated to the point where I wanted to die. After one particularly terrifying night, I could no longer deny the truth. If I wanted to live—I needed to get out. The next morning when he left for work, I also left and that was that.

I had a chronic back problem at the time, and moving even a few boxes left me in excruciating pain. But all the equipment I needed to continue my life as a professional artist was still in my former home, inaccessible after he changed the locks. I was faced with the choice of walking away from my profession as an artist or fighting to regain my belongings. I felt trapped into a battle for my stuff, which represented my ability to make a living. I was trapped by the limits of my body and my dependence on those things. And that was when I realized that real freedom for me would mean owning a lot less stuff.

v a n   d w e l l i n g

After the toxicity of my former life, I found freedom invigorating. I wanted even more freedom. I wanted to do some stealth camping and live in plain sight. This was the most liberated life I could imagine. So I bought a used van and named it "Vincent, my Van that Goghs." I paid a friend to look it over and tune it up (which cost more than the van). I got busy making it nice inside. I built a bed across the back and put shelves on the side. I put down a nice cork floor with a rag rug. I constructed a little low-tech sink set up. I had a jump box that would charge my phone and power a few simple things at night. I even had a "Luggable Loo" for a toilet. I was timidly ready to give this van dwelling life a shot.

I did some camping and boondocking, and took care of pets when friends were out of town. I loved falling asleep under the stars and hearing the wild noises outside my van. I was developing a whole new set of skills. I found out that I could be very comfortable overnight in the van even when temperatures were as low as 29 degrees Fahrenheit. I loved that I could get off work in the evening and go anywhere, taking my home with me, though I usually didn't. I had work and family that kept me in the area. My van, which I soon called "Vinnie" for short, was a symbol of possibility parked right outside my little apartment. Someday soon, I was going to take the leap and become a full-time van dweller!

I met a man, and he was handsome. But more surprisingly, he was kind. I enjoyed his laughter and his company. I thought I'd at least stick around until he was tired of being kind, then I would move on. However, he never did forget to be kind because it wasn't an act. In fact, everything about him drew me in. I had given up on marriage, on being a part of a couple, on all of it. But here he was, this kind, brilliant, inventive, and handsome man—rocking my world.

One day, I accidentally asked him to marry me while he was busy washing dishes (as any smart woman would). With a twinkle in his eye, a toss of his imaginary long hair, and in his best falsetto he declared, "I won't say yes until I see the ring!" I got the plastic ring off my bottle of ginger ale and put it on his finger and we dissolved into laughter and kisses—we were engaged.

a new beginning

We soon married, moved into a small, 650-square-foot house, and set about renovating his deli into a restaurant. We refinished the hardwood floors, built bathrooms, and painted. We built all new plumbing and electrical systems and bought a bunch of shiny new restaurant equipment. Using his antiques and a glorious old Steinway grand piano, we made the place beautiful. We opened the doors and made a crowd of new friends and had a great time preparing and presenting delicious food. We were living the dream—providing scrumptious food and hosting elegant concerts in the restaurant—and it was amazing.

After a while, he was pulled back into his other business while I ran the restaurant. He was traveling a lot. I was working crazy hours running the restaurant, and he was busy restoring instruments. We were missing each other. I had just found him, and I didn't want to live a life separate from his. Even though we loved the restaurant and all the amazing people that we met during that adventure, we closed the place and put the building up for sale. It sold quickly, and we were finally together and free.

chapter 2
purposeful simplicity

Soon after selling the restaurant, we purchased a 125-square-foot tiny home and moved in. I went from having a spacious restaurant kitchen with all the equipment and gear you can imagine to living in sardine-tin-like quarters. Trying to make a meal in an extremely small space was challenging. I didn't have a dishwasher, and there was no space for a food processor, KitchenAid, or the rest of the gear. Further complicating matters, the electricity for our whole home came through a single regular household outlet in our friend's garage, 100 feet away. Our entire house was working on a 15-amp breaker. Even if we had space for fancy gear, we didn't have the power to run it—not if we wanted heat. I really felt the loss of the things I couldn't have because of the limited space and power.

When you transition from one kind of normal to a new and different normal, there are inevitably some uncomfortable patches. You can't take a full-sized life and expect to cram it into a "fun-sized" space with no changes or challenges. This change is about far more than just giving away your shoes and deciding which composting toilet is right for you. Even though I knew our new home was all about liberty, it was impossible to deny that there were times it felt more like poverty.

But poverty and simplicity are not the same thing. Poverty is about lack. Simplicity is about purposeful choices to edit, reduce, and simplify. It may look the same to someone on the outside, but that's beside the point. We chose voluntary, purposeful simplicity in our new tiny life. How could I embrace that life, including all of its difficulties, instead of fighting it? It is a matter of attitude. If you focus on the poverty and deprivation in your situation, you'll be miserable. If you choose instead to make it about simplicity, cooking can once more be a joy. People have cooked simply for generations, without all the electrical equipment. Changing my focus by embracing simplicity helped me make peace with my new tiny life.

simplicity

Simplicity is a choice to create a better life and a more purposeful existence. It's up to us to tell ourselves the truth. We choose to remind ourselves that living tiny is not about poverty, it's about embracing simplicity. Simplicity is a mindset, and one that really matters. Either the mindset changes or living tiny feels like punishment and sacrifice. The more sacrificial it feels, the less likely it is that the changes will last. Changing my mindset to purposeful simplicity was the key to happily living tiny.

Suddenly I was in this tiny kitchen learning to cook a completely different way. When I stepped back and took a good look at what was happening, I realized that I was making food the old-school way. I was working with little more than a cutting board, a good knife, and a gas range. For all my years of experience, I was learning to cook all over again. Great food, simply prepared.

Equipment can make food faster, but it doesn't make food better. I learned to embrace the time involved in making authentic food. Using only basic tools was a way of connecting to the generations of cooks before me. Pioneers cooked over an open fire on their way west. Many generations of women and men cooked over a fire in a kitchen that was just a fireplace and a table. My Mennonite grandparents took their food seriously. My mother's father was a chef when he met my grandmother, and she was a waitress in charge of the service staff at the time. My grandmother on my father's side cooked hearty meals for farm hands during the Great Depression, and for some it may have been the only meal they had all day. As I learned to cook with simplicity and purpose, I connected myself to people who worked hard and enjoyed great food. By embracing simplicity, we created a space that was authentically connected to the past, and yet fully in the present.

wait it out

Anytime you embark on grand changes, there will be some moments in the transition that are uncomfortable. Developing a new normal takes time. When you are tired and frustrated and really feeling the annoyance of the process, just talk yourself down off the ledge and wait it out. It sounds simplistic, but it's still true: wait it out. You will develop a new normal, a new comfort zone— it just takes time. You are creative, determined, and adaptable. You are going to be fine.

creativity & adaptability

We often tell ourselves we are not creative, but it's never true. If you are willing to consider the idea of living tiny, you are creative. Creativity is one of my favorite aspects of living in a tiny house. When you hit a wall with something you're trying to do, creativity and determination will help you find your way around, or over, or under that wall. Your creativity and adaptability are your best assets, and living tiny will help you grow and expand those skills. And that's a very good thing.

chapter 3
low tech

My tall, handsome husband, Xaver Wilhelmy, is a certified pipe organ builder. Until the modern jet airplane of the 1950s, pipe organs were the most complex machines made. There are acoustics, art, electronics, math, physics, plumbing, pneumatics, science, and finesse involved in building these instruments—they are truly marvelous. I've often been moved by the music of the pipe organ. Especially since pipe organs are rare in Mennonite congregations so the music feels especially rare and wonderful to me. More recently, I've found myself admiring the inner workings of these amazing machines. As I become more involved with pipe organs, I am amazed at the vast variety of low-tech mechanical actions they entail. Of course there are highly computerized versions as well, and even faux organs that don't even move air. But those aren't the least bit interesting. I think it's really exciting to see complex things done without the use of electrical power or electronics. Imagine the difference for millions of people if we knew how to survive comfortably without electrical power? Imagine rebuilding after a disaster if off-grid skills were our normal skills and our normal tools didn't have to be plugged in. Imagine the freedom we'd have if we were not tethered by cords and pipelines, but instead, we moved with the wind and soaked up the sun? Something as marvelous and magical as a pipe organ has inspired me to find more low-tech solutions for our own home. Xaver and I wish to live a low-tech life outside the power grid, and as tiny-house dwellers, this is more possible than ever.

As a people, we Americans quickly got used to

having hair dryers and food processors. It wasn't that long ago that people were scrubbing laundry on a rock on the banks of the river. Even more recently people talked to each other through wall mounted telephones with long cords attached to receivers. Before we had all of our modern gear, work still got done. People still cooked amazing meals. Folks still had beautiful gardens. People got around in vehicles that were relatively simple. Plus you could fix the auto on your own under a shade tree.

Sometimes low-tech is less vulnerable to the fluctuations of electric power or fossil fuel availability. And it doesn't require a specialist to fix or maintain it. Sometimes low-tech is more reliable. Low-tech is less affected by social and political unrest. Did I mention pipelines? Things have been done in low-tech ways for generations, and all of a sudden modern times and marketing gurus taught us that we need a gadget or a spray for everything. When, actually, we don't. Stepping outside that system is a powerful statement of liberation and personal resilience. Our sense of "need" is based on what we're used to. But when you change what you are used to, it will change what you need.

When I get frustrated that I don't have what I want and get caught up in a poverty mentality, I remember my roots. My parents were raised on Mennonite farms where they worked together to raise animals for food. They worked together to make and plant a garden, and worked to harvest and preserve the fruits of their labors. They worked hard, but they also had a sense of accomplishment when they came together around a table. They had real skills that translated into real food, nourishment, self-reliance, and strength. They worked hard and it's not too difficult to imagine that their life was a good life, and the fresh, honest food they put on the table was as good as it gets. They ate "farm to fork" cuisine long before it was even a trend. They chose to pass that desire for a high-quality life on to my generation, and I'm glad they did. You don't have to be sentimental about the past to appreciate the quality of locally sourced food our ancestors enjoyed. There is a lot from the past that needs to stay there, but the way food was grown only a few yards from the kitchen table is something that can inspire us. The way the community came together to plant, harvest, and preserve food is also something to inspire us.

We have thousands of products available to us these days, but I wonder if this keeps us from knowing the same sense of fulfillment that my family felt. Sometimes it is necessary for us to look at our lives and consider: with all the products we choose to consume but not to produce, what have we really gained? Do we miss the growing and learning involved in gaining real-life skills and experience? When we're surrounded by manufactured stuff, does it not suggest poverty rather than wealth? The more that we are insulated from self sufficiency by our technology, the more vulnerable we become when systems expand or contract, as they always do.

It's okay to have a kitchen faucet that doesn't require electrical power for fancy touch-sensitive functions. A regular faucet is a wonderful, low-tech device that doesn't need power to work beautifully. Why add power dependency to something that simply works just on the laws of physics? It's okay to use a "Luggable Loo" rather than spend an extra grand on a toilet that does little more than turn ten pounds of waste into ten pounds of waste. It's okay to spend more for the authentic version instead of buying the cheap plastic one. It's good to purchase an item made by an artisan rather than some cheap mass-produced and mass-marketed product. It's okay to choose the simpler version rather than the latest version. It's okay to choose less sometimes—not because we are less, but because we are more. We are not plastic. We choose not to surround ourselves with all that is cheap, fake, and disposable because we are not cheap, fake, and disposable. We pull ourselves out of the need for the latest and greatest and look for the simpler option. We are people of purpose and value. Our time matters, our focus matters, our lives matter. Our sense of calling and vision for the future matter—it all matters. Living simply is about taking hold of a sense of authenticity and purpose, and letting the rest fall away.

Billions of marketing dollars are aimed at your eyes at nearly every moment of every day. The sole purpose of all that is to convince you of what you lack so that you'll buy the product. This feeds the fear that we not only don't have enough, but that we are not enough. Shame is a powerful way to manipulate people and we need to recognize it when it's aimed at us—and resist. It's empowering to turn off that noise. Living in purposeful simplicity is revolutionary. Turn off the messages that shame you. Welcome the silence. Stare down the fear. You are valuable. You matter.

chapter 4
equilibrium

When making big life changes, sometimes we go looking for rules and guidelines to have as a framework for judging our progress. If your goal is to become a minimalist, you may wonder aloud how many dinner plates a minimalist would have. The truth is that some have lots, and some have only one per person. Wanting to know the magic number of plates everyone "should" have isn't about some universal truth or even the magic of letting go: it's about perception. And any time we start accepting "should" or the vernacular "yaneedta" from strong external voices, we start to lose our own.

The goal is not to get down to owning only 100 items. The goal is not to see how small you can get your living space. Simplicity is not a competition or comparing ourselves to someone else. It is not just the opposite extreme from consumerism—though we are drawn to extremes and might have to go through the opposite one. We often start out as materialists because that is the path our culture opens for us. But when that doesn't satisfy, we swing hard for minimalism. But isn't that still an over-emphasis on stuff? Finally, we let an edited group of very special things creep back into our lives as we reach a place of equilibrium. Equilibrium is simplicity, having neither too much nor too little, but everything for a purpose.

The thing is, all too often we don't have a sense of purpose about our lives. If we don't have a sense of vision for the future and goals we are working toward, it's easy to lose our focus and get distracted by mere details. Finding simplicity requires first finding purpose and stocking your life to meet that purpose. Then let the rest fall away.

j o y

Marie Kondo suggests approaching each item with the question: "does it spark joy?" I understand. I have a skein of yarn that brings me joy. I walked into a beautiful boutique yarn store and did what I always do: I stopped and looked around the space to find the best yarn for weaving. Finally, I came to a skein of yarn in a color that always speaks to me. And this one was rich and vibrant and hit me right in the sweet spot. When I reached out and touched that skein of yarn, I found a bewildering softness. It was amazing. The owner of the shop and I had been happily chatting and I held up the yarn and asked, "What is this wonder?"

She smiled a knowing smile and told me of a place in Tibet where the indigenous people dug up their land looking for a specific truffle-like-thing. Whatever this item was, it sold for a high price on the Chinese market. But the constant digging and searching was destroying the land. Workers came and taught the people how to tend the land and grow a very fluffy ox known as a Yak. They harvested the silken down of these amazing animals, dyed it drop-dead-gorgeous colors, and spun it into luxurious yarn. They were sent off to boutique yarn shops all over the world. The money they made selling this glorious yarn was enough to start sending some of their young women off to college. For the first time in memory, the land was growing plants, the community was thriving, and the women were introduced to opportunities they wouldn't otherwise have had. Tears came to my eyes as I heard her tell this story. She bought the yarn for her shop because it was beautiful and it had purpose that aligned with her own. Of course I bought the yarn, and I would do it again even if it meant I was eating rice for a month!

It wasn't the yarn that brought me joy, though it is amazing in its own right. Rather, it's the connection between the purpose of the yarn and my own. This yarn was a means to heal the earth and provide young women with the education they need to succeed. This connects with my own desire that women have opportunities to succeed. This connects also with my desire to see the earth healed from the damage we've done. This is life-purpose that connects with my own. And that's what I see when I look at this yarn. A shared connection. A shared sense of purpose.

purpose

This is all deeper than the question "Does it bring me joy?" will ever reach. "Does it align with my purpose?" is a different question. If the answer is yes, it is likely that it will also bring joy. Joy and happiness are only side effects, not an end in themselves. Purpose is the focus. Being beautiful is enough purpose for some things. Being useful is enough purpose for other things. In my 125-square-feet tiny haven home I keep things that fit my purpose.

No matter what brought you to living tiny, the specific reason doesn't matter. Even if poverty visits your life for a season, there is no shame in that. I hope this book gives you strategies for walking through poverty to purposeful simplicity, because simplicity is liberating.

chapter 5
mise en place

"A place for everything,
everything in its place."
—Benjamin Franklin

There is a cooking practice, called mise en place [mi zã 'plas] which means putting each ingredient in place before you begin cooking. This is a classical approach to cooking used by professionals to have every ingredient ready to go at the beginning of service. For example, instead of having a bell pepper, a chef would have a container of bell pepper cut precisely the way she or he prefers. Television cooking shows sometimes do this: every ingredient—even each spice—will be placed out on the counter in darling little bowls. This preparedness and efficiency allows one to enjoy the unrushed art of cooking.

In a tiny house, keeping a supply of cute little dishes on hand isn't realistic, but neither is it necessary. The beauty of a tiny kitchen is that you may set it up much like a chef sets up the kitchen before service. Everything can be right in its place, and right within reach. The fact that a kitchen is small is a sort of forced efficiency that guarantees that every ingredient and tool is close at hand, even if you don't prep every single ingredient before you begin cooking. I love the efficiency of tiny house cooking. I love how everything is within easy reach in my tiny kitchen.

When I design and build my next small kitchen, I would still design a space where everything is right at hand like the controls of an airplane. And while I am a minimalist, this way of designing a kitchen may not look like minimalism. However, it's incredibly efficient. In a very small kitchen, it's not the style or aesthetic that matters, it's the usefulness and efficiency of the space. This may mean giving up that ultra-clean and empty minimalist style in favor of having everything right in reach. Small kitchen efficiency is a sort of built in "mise en place" that makes cooking a joy.

chapter 6
right-sizing

Moving your household from an ordinary house into a tiny home on wheels, skoolie, van, or RV is the best move you'll ever make. When was moving as simple as parking one home beside the other and walking back and forth while you put your favorite things in place? With a home on wheels, any time you are "moving" will mean moving your entire home as a unit. This is much simpler than another visit into the tumultuous and chaotic world of packing boxes and moving them one by one until every muscle aches. That's one reason tiny house living is the best liberation. The mobile nature of a tiny home, skoolie, van, or RV makes it possible to park one next to the other, and get on with the work. It's the easiest way to move!

Once you've decided to go tiny, start sharing things you don't use. Long before you decide whether you'll build your tiny home yourself or place an order for one, you can begin going tiny. Even before you choose what kind of composting toilet is right for you, donate everything in your attic. Start getting rid of duplicates. Give decorative things to anyone who has admired them. Start early so that you can take your time.

It's good to work on sorting and decision making for up to two hours a day (any longer will risk decision fatigue). Not everyone will have the luxury of working that slowly, but where an individual has lived in a home for many years, this process needs to be done gently.

Make a "keep" pile and a "go" pile, nothing in between. A "maybe" pile will only mean moving that box again and again. Just take your time, spend a few seconds with each item, and make the call. You won't miss any of it when it's gone. In fact, I've found that I'm far more likely to look at something I kept and wonder why on earth I haven't purged it already.

"Downsizing" is a stressful process and puts the focus on getting rid of things, which is painful and invasive. "Downsizing" focuses on loss. "Right-sizing" means liberating your life from the spirit-clogging mass of belongings that keep you trapped and overwhelmed. Focus on the freedom you will find on the other side rather than focusing on the loss of each individual item. Focus on what you gain rather than what won't fit.

Be careful with your loved ones during this process. Don't make something disappear that belongs to someone else. Be respectful of what someone else has difficulty parting with. We love things for various reasons, and keeping things only for sentimental reasons is just a phase we walk through as our purpose becomes more clear. For a while I kept a few things from my grandmother, mainly just because they came from her. I later realized I didn't need 10 different things that came from my grandmother, I chose my favorite one and let the rest go. Bring your favorite elements of your old home into your new home so that you are surrounded only by things you love and will actually touch, see, and use!

When you start to get bogged down, clean up the immediate mess and step aside. Remind yourself why you're going tiny. Remind yourself of the financial savings of living tiny. Stop the downsizing for a while and take care of yourself. Cook something amazing. Read a book. The next day you can get back at it. Your donated items will help someone else. Going tiny is not about sacrifice, or punishment for financial sins. Going tiny is about having your very favorite things close at hand. Going tiny is about liberation. Pure and simple.

donating & selling
https://tinyhousefoodie.com/2018/01/04/day-4-right-sizing-your-kitchen/

chapter 7
gifts

Once you have embarked on the job of right-sizing your home, someone will inevitably (and innocently) want to give you something. Consider what is the most gracious response to such an offer, especially since a person is more valuable than any project or product. Many times, this will mean graciously accepting the gift, even if that means one more thing you have to purge. Nevertheless, always be gracious. Preaching at a generous person about materialism and going tiny is a breach of etiquette. Going tiny is less stressful if you don't turn it into a crusade. Simply add the gift item into your already well-developed purging process. Expecting others to "get it" is too much to ask when the dominant culture is just that—dominant. It wasn't that long ago that you didn't get it, or you wouldn't still be getting rid of schnitzel. Be genuinely gracious. Being rude over stuff is just as bad as being mired under a pile of useless schnitzel.

You've found this path and adopted it for yourself, but it isn't the right path for everyone. It's better to be a magnetic force than a negative, preachy one. Tiny house people are finding liberation in the lightness of their load. Share your story of liberation at every opportunity. Send your sermons to the landfill along with your plastic containers, old spices, and everything in your junk drawer (except the coins and keys).

refuse freebies
One of the most liberating elements of learning to live tiny is that it allows us the freedom to refuse what we do not need. In all truth, living tiny starts outside the

home.

Bea Johnson, in her book *Zero Waste Home*, encourages her readers to refuse single-use plastics, freebies such as hotel room toiletries, party favors, food samples, and swag bags. She has gone to great lengths to stem the flow of junk mail to her mailbox. She brings her own containers and bags when shopping, and will refuse receipts, opting to have them emailed to her instead. Her book on zero-waste living is an excellent resource for tiny house folks looking for ways of handling the constant stream of waste typical of modern American life.

Truth is, if you're moving your tiny home around pretty often, junk mail won't be an issue. If you're on the road in your home, hotel room toiletries won't be an issue either. Refusing freebies offered by a retailer is not difficult. Product packaging and shopping bags are a little more challenging and that's been a process for Xaver and I. In my forthcoming book *Mennonite Clean: The Pure & Simple Green Clean Home* I share much more on my approach to non-toxic cleaning, avoiding trash, and transitioning to more environmentally respectful options. In a tiny house, there is only room for items that are purposeful, and sometimes that means politely declining freebies.

part 2

simple
kitchen
equipment

chapter 8
simple equipment

Since I've gone tiny, I've learned a few things the hard way. I've developed some strategies that will help you. I'll start with a list of gear that you can use as a strategy on your right-sizing journey to a smaller, simpler kitchen.

If you don't cook, you may not be enjoying the level of health and wellness that could be yours. Therefore, the process of going through your kitchen using this gear list can set you up for success as you explore cooking as a way to improve your physical and financial health and to express your creativity.

If you are just starting out life on your own, maybe you aren't sure where to start. This tool list can also help you put together a set of kitchen gear that will serve you well for many years. If you're used to a big kitchen full of specialized equipment but are making a move to a much smaller space, this list is also for you. Really, I wrote this for anyone just starting out, or embarking on Swedish Death Cleaning—and all of us in between.

A tiny house with a small kitchen, outfitted with some variation on the items on this list, will prepare you for vibrant and joyful cooking. This is a list for folks who actually cook. In my case, when I eat out, I often feel sub-par afterwards. Home cooks will often find restaurant food somewhat disappointing. Eating out occasionally and purposefully (not a last-minute choice of convenience or desperation) can be a great way to get out of a food rut, explore new flavors, and celebrate life's milestones. But cooking your own creative meals at home on a regular basis is a great way to ensure that you are enjoying fresh, healthy food created in an environment free of toxins and pathogens. Eating well is all about quality of life and has short- and long-term ramifications for your health. Thus, developing a collection of good-quality gear and a set of good cooking habits are crucial steps toward eating great food most of the time.

It is important to see this gear list as a strategy rather than a set of strict rules. I am offering this kitchen gear list based on minimalist, frugal, off-grid, low-tech, environmentally friendly, and zero-waste values that are not unique to me. Plus, I have lived in 125 square feet for so long that I know this works. Naturally, you may choose to create your kitchen according to your own values and goals and, in that case, you can use this list as a starting point. Begin here and add useful tools as you go along to personalize your kitchen to the unique way that you cook, but remember, it's always easier to gain more gear than it is to get rid of it.

I cook like a North-American, Mennonite artist who goes Paleo from time to time, and my inventive husband cooks like a European who loves wine, cheese, and bread (well—that's who we are). We both cook in an improvisational style based on the ingredients we have available.

how many plates?

For someone who has the goal of visiting every country in the world by the time they are 60 years old, a dinner plate may not even be a useful part of their cooking collection. For someone who has the purposeful goal of cooking for the homeless every week, having dinner plates (or lunch bags, or something similar) is going to be important. In fact, plates are just plates and they are only needed if they serve a purpose. I think it helps if they are both useful and beautiful. (Because beauty is an often overlooked need in our lives.) It is good to have what we need to fulfill our sense of purpose, and let the rest go. That's the basic reality of the right-sizing process and it may not always feel comfortable, but it is definitely purposeful. The Tiny House Foodie equipment list isn't a rule, it's a strategy that starts in a sense of purpose. Start here and find your own place of balance and beauty.

find your why
https://tinyhousefoodie.com/2018/01/01/day-1-right-sizing-your-kitchen-in-2018/

choose your favorites
https://tinyhousefoodie.com/2018/01/02/day-2-right-sizing-your-kitchen-in-2018/

chapter 9
dinnerware

The perfect tiny house plate is a small one. I would recommend a plate that is between seven and eight inches in diameter. These small plates fit in small storage spaces and more people can enjoy a meal at a small table if the plates are fairly small. Plus, it is easier to control portion sizes with a smaller plate. You can always go back for seconds, but at least the first helping won't be over-sized.

How many plates to own? The simplest answer is one per person in the household. In a tiny house without a dishwasher, there is no need to have a battalion of plates so that you don't run out of clean dishes before it is time to run the dishwasher again. In a tiny house, you wash dishes after every meal and put them in the drainer to dry, and use them again for the next meal. What could be simpler? If you'd like to start out with more than one per person, that's fine. In six months, when you have determined which plates you actually use, donate the others to lighten the load.

A plate may also be used as a lid on top of a bowl for food storage. Or you can place a bowl upside down on the plate for another food storage option. This reduces both the need for additional food storage containers and the need for plastics and single-use wraps.

A year or so ago I came across a set of beautiful china dishes at an antique store for an insanely low price. Having a weakness for all things delicate, well made, and beautiful, I longed to buy them, but since I was an aspiring minimalist, I left without purchasing them.

Xaver and I talked about it and, after a month or so, we went back for them and made this our Christmas gift to ourselves. We now keep two of these small plates, two bowls, and two teacups and saucers in our tiny house and we are delighted to eat off of beautiful china each day. I have the rest of the set boxed away in storage and if something breaks, I'll go to storage and pull out another piece, no problem. Using these dishes brings me the joy that we are making each day a celebration.

Some will advise that you choose the best quality plates you have, but it is not necessary to pick the newest, best, or most expensive of your plates. The distinction of "everyday" or "good" dishes is one made by marketers to sell more plates, otherwise the idea is of no real use. The ones you choose don't even have to match. Choose your favorites, the ones you will most enjoy using.

Automatically toss out melamine or plastic plates, since they just aren't worth the potential health risks. Discard any dishes that are chipped, broken, or stained. Also, toss any plates that have a negative memory attached to them, as there is no room in a tiny house for such things.

The idea of keeping disposable plates and napkins in a tiny house is counterproductive. Disposables take up a lot of space, they are very expensive, and they're one slice of pizza away from the landfill. It's just not worth it. If you entertain, keep a few extra plates on hand or borrow plates from a neighbor when needed. Use up disposables and embrace the honest simplicity of doing dishes. Savy marketing promises that paper plates simplify life because it saves time cleaning up, but is it really that difficult to wash a plate?

right-sizing plates & bowls
https://tinyhousefoodie.com/2018/01/08/right-sizing-plates-and-bowls/

b o w l s

Choose the bowls you use the most (unless the bowl you always use is plastic). In our case, we chose a pair of china-rimmed soup bowls. I also keep a pair of large coffee/soup mugs. There is something so cozy and comforting about a large mug of soup on a cold winter's day. Even though the portion size is the same for the bowls and mugs, I keep them both because I use them both. The bowls can serve salad, fruit, popcorn, or soup. Some folks may choose to use a glass measuring cup for a bowl, since this is a real multipurpose item. There is no wrong answer here.

There is also no need for all your plates and bowls to match. In fact, an eclectic, mismatched combination might be a better expression of your individuality. A friend of ours purchased vintage plates at thrift stores for her intimate wedding; afterward she kept her favorites and her friends and family snagged their favorites as well. Pick your favorites and share the rest. Follow the simple strategy that when you bring a new favorite into your home, an old favorite is given away. In this way, we keep the space we gain in our lives through right-sizing.

g l a s s w a r e

Gone are the days when there is a specific glass for a specific drink. Say farewell, that ship has sailed. Choose glasses that work for wine, iced tea, water, or whatever your drink of choice is. If you have very little cabinet space, you might choose stemless glasses. Or, you can choose to use stemware for everything and mount a wine glass rack under a kitchen shelf. Keep your favorite glasses and share the rest.

We keep a little collection of mismatched wine glasses that we've purchased at thrift stores. We tend to choose hand-blown ones that are a little wonky and we usually pay less than 50 cents for each one, so if one is broken, it is no great loss. We also have two beautiful, mismatched, etched antique shot glasses (stamperl) that are prefect for schnapps or grappa. Any of these glasses also work nicely for a few fresh blooms. We have a small glass rack made of metal that holds about a dozen glasses. It is mounted under the cabinet right over our kitchen sink. We wash a glass by hand, and put it in the wine glass holder to drain directly into the sink. Details like this are possible in small kitchens and it's one of the reasons why tiny kitchens are so efficient and fun.

right-sizing glassware
https://tinyhousefoodie.com/2018/01/09/right-sizing-glassware-day-7/

f l a t w a r e
I keep three mugs on the kitchen counter against the back splash, one for knives, one for forks, and one for spoons. Only items that are used every day are kept on the counter-top, and flatware and utensils certainly qualify.

Once in our travels we came across an antique store with a booth selling old silver-plated flatware. I was fascinated by the endless choices in patterns and styles. From then on, we have used mismatched silver in our home. I have a number of pieces that came from my grandparents and I was happy to add those to the mix. It is my theory that you can never have too many spoons (minimalist, huh?), especially if you are doing a lot of taste testing in the kitchen, but, as always, specific quantities are up to you. Choose your favorite flatware, whether new or old, stainless or silver, matching or not, and share the rest.

right-sizing flatware
https://tinyhousefoodie.com/2018/01/10/right-sizing-flatware-day-8/

right-sizing utensils
https://tinyhousefoodie.com/2018/01/23/right-sizing-utensils-day-17/

chapter 10
cutlery

knives

I'm a retired chef and restaurant owner. I have beautiful knives, a whole set, and I enjoy using them. However, the knives we actually use in our tiny house are a small 6.5-inch chef's knife and a three-inch paring knife. I rarely use any other knives. I find this pretty amusing, to be honest. Good knives are very expensive, and a good one has a great feeling in the hand. I know all that, yet here I am, day after day, reaching for a cheap, pink, miniature chef's knife. It's hilarious. My Austrian sharpens this knife when needed. I suspect I paid only $14 for my little Japanese knife, and it is a great multi-purpose knife. Our nephew even opened a metal can with it once.

If you think you can't live without lots of additional knives, give it a try. You might be surprised. If you have room and don't mind the investment, a longer, good quality chef's knife is useful for larger fruits and vegetables. A serrated knife is useful for bread, tomatoes, and the occasional steak. If you have other knives that you use for specific tasks, and you use them more than once a month, add them to your tiny house collection. Share the rest.

Store knives on a magnetic knife strip near your cutting board. Sometimes this is as simple as sticking the knife strip to the side of the fridge, and the knives go onto the strip. Some strips require a slightly more complicated installation. Knife blocks take up too much space and may be unsanitary.

It is useful to have a pair of kitchen shears. Pick a tough pair that will last a long time. These can be stored on the magnetic strip with the knives or in a canister with utensils.

cutting boards

We have a large (12 x 18 x 1.5 inch), substantial cutting board that works for cutting produce and carving proteins. It works as a trivet to protect our little walnut two-top dining table from the heat of a pan. It fits over the sink to expand our counter top area. Plus, in a pinch it can also be used as a tray to carry a few items out to the rocket stove for al fresco cooking. Choose your favorite wooden or bamboo board for your own health and safety, and avoid plastic.

cutting boards & knives
https://tinyhousefoodie.com/2018/01/11/right-sizing-cutting-boards-knives-day-9/

chapter 11
cookware & bakeware

the dutch oven

Ages ago I purchased a 4.5 quart "Le Creuset" Dutch oven, and also the metal lid knob so I could use the lid in the oven. It is one of the best kitchen investments I've ever made. It started out blue, but we used it on the rocket stove so often that it's black on the outside. No worries, it will clean up beautifully when I get around to giving it a good scrub. This enamel-coated cast-iron cookware is virtually indestructible and should be considered a purchase for life, not just for now. "Staub" is another brand, and "Lodge" is a budget friendly brand of cast iron Dutch ovens that are available in many sizes and colors.

Choose your favorite color, that way it will out-last your choice of kitchen decor. And get one that is the right size for you. The 4.5 quart is perfect for the pair of us, even when we cook up something to last us a couple of days or have guests.

A Dutch oven (also called a French oven) is useful for baking bread, making soup, and the heat retention of cast iron makes it perfect for searing your favorite protein. It's also the basis for my "fireless cook-er." (For more information about the fireless cooker, see my forthcoming book *Home Unplugged: Simple Off-Grid Solutions*.) Time and time again I reach for this simple piece of cooking gear to make all sorts of recipes in quantities from small to large. Chose the size and color that is right for you. One is all you need. Put the Dutch oven into your oven or on your range while not in use. Done.

s a u c e p a n & s k i l l e t

Select your favorite saucepan and skillet. If the non-stick coating is coming off, or the handle is loose, donate it. Shop at a kitchen store for a new one that is light and well-balanced, yet also has a solid base for heat distribution. Notice the angle of the handle, as professional models are designed to keep the chef's hand further from the flame, but this may be an uncomfortable angle for a home cook in a compact kitchen. Do get the matching glass lid. This is not something you should buy online unless you've had a chance to get a feel for the product and find the one that is right for you.

I've recently looked at skillets and saucepans in my favorite brands and was surprised by how heavy they are. When living on tires, it is helpful to notice how much weight these items add to the home, especially if you will be moving at times. In addition, heavier cookware is more wearing for the cook. But if your favorite is a cast iron skillet, keep it. There is no better skillet. When moving our home, I sometimes pack some heavier items into my car. Lightening the load for the trip can't hurt.

I've kept an eight-inch skillet for at least two years in our tiny home. I've recently added a 10-inch skillet that is perfect for making omelets, and I like that one better. There isn't enough difference between the two to keep them both, so I've decided to just keep the larger one and share the other.

Don't feel that you need to purchase a set that has items in it that you won't use and don't have room for. Rather, choose your components on a case-by-case basis. (There is no need for these items to match.) Create your very own set. Do purchase reputable brands that are made with good quality metal.

Pots and pans are real space hogs in kitchen cabinets, so it is best to hang them. (When the house is on the move, take them down and pack them with dish towels in the sink.) One can hang pots from pegboard, and purchase hooks online rather than a box store where they are expensive. Julia Child hung her collection of beautiful French copper pots on pegboard.

Who can argue with her?! You can purchase an overhead pan rack or up-cycle something to that purpose. There are also bars that can be mounted on the wall under cabinets/shelves for handy storage. If the tiny house "mother-ship" known as Ikea is too far from you for a pilgrimage, a curtain rod or an interesting looking bathroom towel bar may work just as well. Just be sure to mount it into real wood so that it doesn't fall off the wall at three a.m., waking you from a sound sleep, and causing you to hit your head on the ceiling in the loft, especially if that's going to cause you to swear in several languages. That would just be preposterous!

right-sizing pots & pans
https://tinyhousefoodie.com/2018/01/12/right-sizing-pots-pans-day-10/

b a k e w a r e
A pair of cookie sheets that fit your oven are useful for baking cookies and roasting vegetables, and toasting nuts. A glass or ceramic baking dish is helpful for roasting and baking, and can double up as a storage container for potatoes and onions when not in use. Cupcake/muffin tins can often be found at thrift shops for those who like to bake, if you use them often enough to justify the space they require.

right-sizing bakeware
https://tinyhousefoodie.com/2018/01/17/right-sizing-baking-gear-day-13/

chapter 12
coffee & tea

drinkware
We have two enormous mugs that hold roughly 16 ounces of coffee or tea. We also keep two beautiful china tea cups and the matching saucers. Xaver has a coffee travel cup with a lid that is good for taking a cup of coffee with him.

coffee
When I met my handsome husband, he had a very complex coffee machine on his kitchen counter. It made a lot of mildly disturbing noises and spit out small cups of strong, dark, fragrant bitter-bean-juice. It also had a few other interesting functions that I never really understood because I'm not a coffee person. I did finally learn how to make a non-objectionable cup for him from time to time, but it was overly complex and a nuisance to clean.

In our tiny home there is no room for fancy gear, and that fancy machine died before we went tiny anyway. These days my handsome man still has his coffee ground to an espresso grind, and after some trial and error, he's found the true tiny house coffee-making routine that works for him. He puts a heaping teaspoon of coffee grounds in his coffee mug, and pours boiling water from the tea kettle in on top. He lets the cup sit for a bit, and sometimes he stirs just the top with a fork. Once the floating grit has all settled to the bottom, he drinks his delightfully strong, super-simple coffee—all but the last gritty swallow at the bottom. One of us will add a bit of water to the cup at that point, and usually throw the gritty contents straight out the front door into the wilderness of wild raspberries and walnut trees that surround our tiny haven home. When we're at work, those grounds are more likely to go in a designated compost pile (and sometimes they're just thrown over the porch rail in the general direction of the compost pile). Coffee grounds are good for the garden, so no worries. What could be simpler? Fresh, fragrant coffee, using only a whistling tea kettle, a mug, a container to keep your ground coffee (a quart-size mason jar works great), and a spoon that lives with the coffee. Super simple.

t e a

My tea routine is similar to my husband's coffee method, but I use a pincer tea strainer. I purchase loose tea. No tea bags are needed. I fill one side of my tea strainer with tea, snap it closed and put it in my tea cup. I fill the cup with hot water from the whistling tea kettle. I have found that if I boil water in a saucepan, I forget it's there. The whistle of the tea kettle helps to remind me what I was doing. Coming back one time to the stove and seeing the fire on under an empty (and extremely hot) sauce pan was a good reminder to use the whistling tea kettle so that I don't burn down my tiny house. That would not be worth saving the space the kettle takes up. I sometimes add a bit of honey from a quart jar that I purchase locally, but to be honest, good tea doesn't even need that.

Sometimes, on a cold winter morning, I treat myself to a very special cup of what can only be considered dessert in a cup. I brew a strong cup of Earl Grey tea (make mine decaf) and pour in a splash of Amarula, available at the American Boy's Club. This is a cream liqueur my Austrian remembers from his time living in South Africa, and he found it at the ABC store and brought it home as a special treat. It's heaven. What a treat for special mornings when we can wake up slow and luxuriate together. If your ABC store doesn't have this one, look for a good eggnog at Christmas time. A little splash of either one in your coffee or tea is a special treat for a cold winter morning. There is no deprivation in our coffee and tea ritual. We drink from fine china cups with saucers, and I stir my tea with a silver spoon.

A good whistling tea kettle has a broad base that comes in full contact with the stove top. I made the mistake of purchasing a very cute round one with much less surface area to connect with the stove top. It takes much longer (and wastes energy) to use that one, so I donated it.

My tall, handsome, Austrian brother-in-law jokes that we live in a "sardine can" and we have laughed a lot over his characterization of our tiny 125-square-foot home. Living in our sardine can is no sacrifice. We have found ways to enjoy luxuries that are specific to the pair of us. Life is what we make of it, and we have chosen to make it a delightful adventure.

tiny house coffee & tea
https://tinyhousefoodie.com/2018/01/15/right-sizing-coffee-tea-day-11/

chapter 13
food preparation

mixing bowls & lids

I love a good prep bowl! I currently use a five-quart stainless-steel mixing bowl in my tiny house, and it's handy to have two of these. I chose a stainless-steel bowl for my tiny home because it's lightweight and indestructible. In addition to food prep, I often fill it with hot soapy water for washing dishes or other things.

Sometimes I use a stainless-steel prep bowl as a temporary kitchen compost catcher. Depending on where we are parked, I may toss scraps right out the front door in true redneck composting glory. It amuses me very much to throw compost scraps into the under-growth of the walnut grove that has become our haven. When we are parked in town or near neighbors, I save scraps in a prep bowl with a silicone cover and take them to a compost pile. I purchased a selection of silicone cookware and bakeware lids and use them every day in place of plastic cling film, plastic storage containers, and aluminum foil. It will take years to wear out these lids and I will have kept piles of disposable items from the landfill. Every bit counts—plus they are cute!

My favorite prep bowl is the Mason Cash mix-ing bowl in bright green, but mine weighs three pounds and ten ounces when empty. This is a great bowl for taking a salad to a party. I also love big glass bowls, and if you are creating food videos, glass may be the best option. However, glass may be even heavier than china or stoneware. If your house is on tires, weight is an issue. If you move your tiny home from place to place pretty often, or intend to travel, go for the stain-less-steel version.

m e a s u r i n g

I use a glass measuring pitcher for measuring and for beating eggs, making dressing, or for other small recipes. I have also used it as a ladle, a soup bowl, gravy boat, and dog food dispenser. Furthermore, it's not a bad vase for flowers. I use it for food storage of leftovers, and simply place a saucer or silicone lid on the top and place it in the fridge. We rarely have leftovers at our house. Between the handsome husband who can eat anything and never gain weight, and a happy puppy dawg, leftovers just don't happen very often.

A set of measuring spoons and cups is not a bad idea, especially if you bake. In a restaurant you have to measure so a recipe can be repeated and remain consistent. Home cooking, however, is very different and I rarely use measuring devices at home. Precision is more important for baking, so that's when measuring spoons and cups come in handy. I prefer to create recipes by weight and convert to measures, but most American recipes are written in measures. Therefore, it's good to have a set of measuring spoons and cups on hand. If you bake, it is good to have a small, good quality kitchen scales for more precise baking.

mixing bowls & lids
https://tinyhousefoodie.com/2018/01/16/right-sizing-mixing-bowls-day-12/

food storage solutions
https://tinyhousefoodie.com/2018/01/18/food-storage-containers-day-14/

chapter 14
appliances - the big three

If you've built your tiny home, or had a builder do the work for you, you may have already chosen your larger kitchen appliances. If you purchased a ready-made option, you may not have many choices to make in this area. And if you're creating a kitchen in a very small home—say 100 square feet or less, chances are you'll be making some challenging decisions about appliances pretty quickly.

In Vinnie 1, a cargo van, I kept a camping stove and an electric cooler. I never cooked inside that van, but kept the gear for camping. In Vinnie 2, we had a gas range with four burners over a small oven powered by propane. This was a cute RV range that I really loved. In addition, we had a small fridge that worked on propane and electrical power—also from the RV market. Since the oven in the range didn't work very well (it was "vintage" after all) we used a toaster oven as well. This was an ideal setup for us for more than three years.

Vinnie 3 is a short-bus turtle shell Skoolie and a little bit smaller than Vinnie 2, so we'll have a small fridge, an induction cooktop, and I may be able to find space for the toaster oven as well.

Because the tiny house movement is highly individualized and many homes are DIY, there is a broad range of what appliances home owners have designed into their homes. Some have found smaller units, or units built for the RV market. Some tiny house kitchens lack nothing an ordinary kitchen has.

oven

I have a counter-top oven and I use it instead of a microwave. Use whatever sort of oven is the best for your situation, and try to create space for it somewhere other than on the counter-top. Remove any duplicate ovens. One is plenty.

Be very aware of where your oven is placed and if it has good ventilation. Be sure that nothing flammable is nearby. Keep cookbooks, cereal boxes, and the like away from the oven. In a tiny house, baking a pan of cookies can warm the whole house, which can be pleasant in the winter but unwelcome the rest of the time. Therefore, I bake only one oven-full of cookies at a time and freeze the rest of the dough so that the oven is only on for a short time. I don't bake things that require long oven times because I don't want to over-heat the cabinet where my oven resides.

refridgerator

Another appliance that takes a lot of space and power in the kitchen is the fridge. We lived without a refrigerator for a portion of the time we lived tiny, and during that time we acquired the habit of not buying a lot of things that need fridge space. It wasn't as difficult as you'd think.

After a few years, we purchased a workshop for our business and it came with a small kitchen that had a really big fridge. We removed the monster-fridge and replaced it with two small, under-counter models. We knew we didn't need the big one and it was an energy drain and space hog. Plus, the small kitchen felt much more spacious without the huge fridge. We have not regretted this move!

Europeans already use under-cabinet fridges, and I love the look of a kitchen without the big presence of a large fridge. There are just two of us, and we don't want to pay the energy bill to cool space we aren't using. Plus, have you ever noticed how much noise a fridge makes?

If you are a vegetarian or vegan, you will quickly

find that you need very little refrigerated space. If you don't drink sugary sodas in single-use plastic containers, you'll save a lot of space. Even if you enjoy a bottle of beer or white wine from time to time, there is no need to fill the fridge with more of these bottles than can be used in a day or two. Use a smaller fridge and stock it as needed.

Another key to using a smaller fridge is to get rid of all the jars of sauces and stop buying new ones. Make your own sauces with avocado, egg, olive oil, and vinegar, and the addition of herbs, spices, and essential oils. I've gotten in the habit of making a dressing for a salad in the bowl before I add the greens and other ingredients. That way I make only enough to dress the salad I'm making, and I can make the dressing flavor profile different each time, which makes eating salads much more interesting. Plus, that way I know I'm using only fresh, healthy ingredients.

tiny house refrigeration
https://tinyhousefoodie.com/2017/11/30/refrigera-tion-in-a-tiny-house/

d i s h w a s h e r

As a normal part of the downsizing process, kiss the dish-washing machine goodbye. Dishwashers are loud energy and water hogs, add extra steps to the cleaning rituals of kitchen life, and don't even get the dishes clean all of the time. The only good thing about a dishwasher is the opportunity to hide dirty dishes out of sight, and you can do that in a regular cabinet (wait, what?!) or just wash them.

Have you ever noticed the hazardous chemical warning on the dish-washing detergent? Why would one "wash" dishes with toxins?! People in my family wash the dishes before they go in the dishwasher, so one wonders why there is even a need to wash them the second time.

Did you know that the most common reason for home insurance claims is from water damage caused by a leak to or from the dishwasher? (The other culprit is the water line to the ice machine on the fridge.) The leak is hidden while it is happening, so by the time it is discovered the damage may be extensive. As you down-size from a large home to a more modest one, say good-bye to the dishwasher. You will enjoy the peace and quiet.

chapter 15
small appliances

I have lived in a tiny house of 125 square feet for three years with no room for much in the way of small kitchen appliances. At first I found this frustrating. I would say to myself, "If I had my [fill in the blank] here I would make [fill in the blank]," and sigh with dramatic frustration and waste my energy on feeling wretched. But as soon as I embraced my creativity and adaptability, I found new solutions and got right back to making great food.

Over time I discovered that I could actually make most of the things I wanted to make without having space-and-energy-sucking appliances. There is even an advantage in not having to clean up the gear after I made the food. I washed the simple tools, put them away, and that was it. No big mess, no detailed scrubbing, no reassembly, no wrestling things in or out of kitchen cabinets. Not only was my home lighter, I felt lighter. The simplicity agreed with me. I learned the liberating truth that I can cook the way my grandparents did (my grandfather was a chef in his youth and my grandmother cooked for farm hands during the Great Depression) and their parents before them. I can create great food the way cooks all over the world do every day. I liked that feeling. I still do.

It's not my purpose to talk you out of your favorite kitchen appliance. That isn't a goal of mine, nor would I be successful if it were. Kitchen appliances can be great, fun, and amusing. My goal is to show you that there is a lot of great food that can be created without them, just the way cooks and chefs have done for countless generations. Appliances don't make the food better, and sometimes, when you count the time required to clean, maintain, and store them, they aren't even time-saving. The truth is, many times there is a low-tech, human-powered alternative.

That said, an appliance that you use every day, or even once a month is one that you should consider carefully. You may prefer to turn the large coffee system into a gift for a friend. You may purchase a product that will do various tasks and donate the single-purpose gadgets. If you aren't going off grid or preparing for that contingency, you may still want to consider energy-weight- and space-saving devices for your small kitchen.

Here are some of the most common kitchen appliances (this list is not intended to be exhaustive). Preserving food through canning, dehydrating, fermenting, and freezing requires a whole other set of gear, and there is a wealth of information on these topics at your favorite library. This list is provided to support you through the right-sizing process to purposeful simplicity.

blending & juicing

Instead of an immersion blender, purchase an egg beater. I remember this gadget from my youth and recently came across a nice one in a specialty kitchen store and they can also be found in antique shops. I make beautiful fluffy eggs without the noise of a stick blender, and no need for electrical power. As the gentlemen was checking out my purchases at the beautiful boutique kitchen store in Charlottesville, I held up the egg beater and told him that it was a cordless, off-grid stick blender. He looked shocked but laughed along.

For cooked food, one can use a ricer to puree cooked root vegetables. Next, pass that mixture through a fine mesh strainer to get a puree that is silky-smooth even when you live off grid. It's also possible to use a potato masher for a more rustic puree. A cooked puree is possible without a noisy appliance.

As it happens, the one appliance I have kept in my tiny house all this time was a Ninja Master Prep blender, which is a blender with the power head on the top (avoiding the inevitable mess if a seal breaks). We used them in the restaurant and they proved to be tough machines. Plus, it takes up very little space compared to some of those monster blenders. If I did not already have this product left over from my days as a restaurant owner, or if this one ever wears out, I would not hesitate to buy another.

I have not found an alternative to a blender for making a smoothie with frozen fruit or ice. I make a lot of smoothies in the summer, and using a blender or food processor is still the best way to take a handful of beautiful fresh raw kale, some frozen fruit, and whirl it into a cold, delicious, and healthy drink. If you have a stick blender and a blender, choose the one you use the most and share the duplicate.

I have not found an alternative to the juicer, but do I use that machine at least once a month? I do not. These days I prefer a prepared super-fruit puree, NingXia Red, which is available with a wholesale membership at Young Living. There are no piles of expensive organic vegetables needed, and no mess to clean up afterward. It's ideal! When I want a fresh green juice, there is a charming locally-owned business not far from me that offers smoothies and fresh juices.

blender & juicer
https://tinyhousefoodie.com/2018/01/25/blender-juicer-day-19/

grating & slicing
A food processor will serve all the functions of a blender, plus the options of grating and slicing food quickly. A box grater is good for grating. A mandoline with slicing and grating blades is another great option. These options are quiet, meditative alternatives to a loud space and energy hog food processor. Use whichever suits you best. Either a box grater or a mandoline can be used very effectively off grid and both will reduce the power needed to run your home.

food processor

https://tinyhousefoodie.com/2018/01/24/food-proces-
sor-day-18/

mixing & whipping

For whipping cream, use a whisk and get a workout at the same time. I was surprised at how quick and easy it was to do this by hand. Use your hands or a wooden spoon to combine ingredients and knead bread by hand. Avoid recipes that require creaming butter. I don't have room for a Kitchen-Aid in my tiny kitchen, so I have kept it in storage all these years. I don't own a hand-held mixer because anything I can do with one of these I can do better in my Kitchen-Aid without having to hover over it.

We had a Kitchen-Aid in the restaurant and used it a lot. When we started having to schedule turns with the mixer, we realized it really was time to purchase another one. My Austrian was shopping for a refurbished model for the more affordable price. I happened to peek over his shoulder and saw a photo of one in a beautiful raspberry color. I must have made a noise of appreciation because he turned and looked at me as I marveled at the beauty of the machine. I told him I was sorry for interrupting his work and sent him back to the task of finding a refurbished one. A few days later, the UPS guy dropped off a box that held this amazing bright pink thing. We had agreed to purchase the cheapest one we could find (a refurbished model) but here was a brand-new Artisan Kitchen-Aid in a ridiculously beautiful color in my kitchen proving that there are exceptions to every rule. He'd given me an amazing gift that day by choosing to purchase the one he knew I'd love rather than the ordinary one. Every time I look at the mixer I remember that my Austrian loves me ostentatiously. Therefore there will always be enough room for the Kitchen-Aid.

What does refurbished mean? In the case of the

Kitchen-Aid stand mixer, it appears to mean that it has been cleaned, and the gear inside was replaced. These replacement gears are not difficult to find online, and if you are handy you will be able to replace it yourself. A Kitchen-Aid doesn't wear out, but the gear might, so we keep a packet with a spare gear taped inside the base of our machine.

mixing & whipping
https://tinyhousefoodie.com/2018/01/26/mixing-and-whipping-day-20/

m i c r o w a v e
We've come a long way. Our equipment has become very sophisticated and very powerful. We can now make food very quickly. With all the great inventions and new technology, we've managed to make food faster. However, we have not managed to make food better. That's why it's no sacrifice to me to get rid of a microwave. It's no sacrifice to skip the freezer section of the market where the overly processed microwave "food" is found in all that packaging. It's no sacrifice to cook great meals and reheat them in a saucepan on the stove, or by heating them in the oven. It's no sacrifice to make real popcorn, and buying popcorn kernels is much cheaper than microwave popcorn, and doesn't come with all that extra packaging. It's no sacrifice to make a fresh cup of coffee rather than reheating an old one.

In a tiny house situation, the power a microwave requires may also be a problem since it may overwhelm the system or cause a breaker to flip. Trust me, that always happens when it's cold, rainy, and after dark and one of us has to go out in that weather with a flashlight to get the breaker turned back on! In an off-grid situation, running a microwave may not even be an option because they are such energy hogs. So part of becoming comfortable with tiny house living may include finding other ways to cook food without the use of the microwave.

To heat water, use a whistling kettle. To heat or

reheat food, use a skillet or sauce pan, and add a little extra water if needed. To warm bread, put it in a paper bag and splash a few drops of water on the bag, and warm it in the oven. Or, if you prefer, toast it. Food that is heated in the conventional way is less likely to burn your mouth, and it tastes better. Plus, it's a real win for your health to kick the microwave out of your life.

right-sizing the microwave
https://tinyhousefoodie.com/2018/01/30/micro-wave-day-22/

What you "need" is based on what you're used to. Change what you're used to, and it will change what you need. The best way to make a real change in your kitchen is to boldly make the needed change and get busy adapting. Before long the new way will be completely normal to you, absolutely second nature. This doesn't happen overnight, but it does happen.

chapter 16
other appliances

Finally, we wade through the last of the kitchen appliances, though of course I may not have mentioned your favorite one. Here are a few of my favorites:

bread machine
If you love bread, as many of us do, a bread machine is a fun piece of equipment. However, it is super easy to make "No Knead Dutch Oven Bread" which was one of my favorite things (back when gluten and I were on speaking terms) without needing a bread machine. Making bread isn't difficult at all, but it does take time. A bread machine doesn't change how long it takes to make bread, and it takes up a lot of space. Why not take bread making back from the appliance and enjoy doing what bakers have done for generations? Try making your own bread and see how it feels to pull a beautiful loaf out of the oven. You might find that baking bread is a pleasure you don't want to sacrifice.

panini press
Heat two skillets. Place the sandwich in one and put the other hot skillet on top, being careful to use a hot pad so you don't burn yourself. Add a brick to the top pan if more weight is needed. It's also possible to toast sandwiches on an outdoor grill for great grill marks and smoky flavor. Use a metal lid to weigh them down.

slow cooker
In a tiny house, one must be extra aware of putting

a lot of moisture into the air, which can lead to mold issues. Therefore, I do not recommend the use of a slow cooker in a tiny house. I also do not recommend leaving a pot on the burner to simmer away for a few hours. In a tiny house, moisture is a real issue and one needs to be mindful. Nobody wants to learn this lesson the hard way.

A close cousin to the slow cooker is a fireless cooker, and I explain this option fully in my book *Home Unplugged: Simple Off-Grid Solutions*, which provides a DIY guide to various off-grid cooking gear along with my favorite off-grid recipes.

slow cooker & friends
https://tinyhousefoodie.com/2018/01/31/the-rest-of-the-appliances-day-23/

t o a s t e r
Toast bread in a skillet. You can toast it with butter, which is delicious, and add a little bit of honey—yum! You can toast your bread after lightly spreading it with mayonnaise, which toasts up to a lovely caramelized color and delicious flavor. You can also toast bread dry. Try all of these ways and see what you think. I like all of these options much better than toast from a toaster, which usually ends up very dry.

tiny house toast & panini
https://tinyhousefoodie.com/2018/01/29/toast-and-panini-day-21/

part 3

shopping
&
food
storage

chapter 17
shopping

Shopping for food to use in a tiny house is not that different from shopping for food for a big kitchen, it's just a lot simpler, faster, and easier. The first key strategy is a simple one: Buy only what you have space for. What could be simpler than that?! No more visits to warehouse stores, no need to fill the whole car with bags of groceries, no need to make several trips from the car into the house. It all just got so much easier! Buy what you will eat in the space of one week or less. That's it. Done.

At the beginning of my life in a tiny house, I really struggled with grocery shopping. I felt like I was buying things in smaller packages, spending more money, and dealing with a larger stream of waste as a result. These days I have found my groove and discovered the strategies that work for me.

shop with your space in mind

I purchase basics like potatoes, onions, and sweet potatoes and keep these away from light so the potatoes don't turn green. These can also be kept on the kitchen counter if you keep the potatoes covered. We go through garlic and onions so quickly that we buy them in larger quantities. For potatoes I'm more likely to pick one or two individual potatoes of various kinds rather than buying a whole bag of one kind. I find that we are more likely to be eating fresh potatoes this way, so this is not a sacrifice. Many fresh fruits and vegetables, such as avocados, tomatoes, garlic, citrus, apples, and pears don't need refrigeration, so I buy plenty of these and keep them on a plate stand on my kitchen counter, where they are fine year around. I also purchase berries, cucumbers, greens and other vegetables that should be refrigerated, but I do so sparingly. If it's too delicate to be left out, I only purchase what can be eaten in a day or two.

I don't use the "convenience bags" at the grocery when buying produce and I avoid fruit or vegetables over-packed on a plastic tray covered with plastic wrap. Packaging waste takes up a lot of space in a tiny house, and is just one more thing that requires attention. The best strategy, therefore, is to simply keep waste out of the house to begin with by shopping smart.

farmer's market

Get to know the farmers at your farmer's market and meet them at their booth early to get the best selection. Buying beautiful, organic, chemical-free fruits and vegetables from farmers will connect you to a real economy of honorable people and the earth they love. Since our market is at a distance, I shop there whenever I'm in the neighborhood.

grocery store

Secondly, find the best grocery store in your area for buying produce if you aren't able to get to market or if it is closed during the winter. My closest favorite happens to be a Kroger store, but I have favorites all over. If you can get there in the morning close to the time when the crew is going through and restocking the produce, you'll have some good options to choose from. There is no need to get your hands dirty in the garden if you'd rather not.

Another key strategy is to shop the outer ring of the grocery store. Skip the prepared food in the middle and just buy what is fresh and lovely from the produce section and supplement with proteins, healthy fats, and a bottle of wine. I've adopted the Paleo diet, but my gentlemen loves his bread and cheese, so I also pick out a nice loaf of bread and a block of cheese that I think he'll enjoy. It's amazing how much simpler and faster shopping has become.

I don't really read ingredient labels because I don't buy much food that has those labels. I don't spend any time with coupons because you rarely see coupons for produce. I buy baking supplies at a bulk food store, so I don't even visit the baking aisle. I don't buy bottled sauces because I don't want them taking up space in my fridge and most of them are laden with MSG (my Austrian is allergic to MSG). Shopping just gets easier and easier!

I LOVE the produce section of grocery stores, so I could shop with my eyes and end up with way too much food to eat in a week simply because the fruits and vegetables that are in season are so appealing that I lose my head in the store. I LOVE the farmer's market and I used to shop for our restaurant, so I can have significant quantities of beautiful fresh produce in my hands without even noticing. These days, I think specifically about what is in my cart and try not to over purchase. And if we run out of something and it's a few days until we go shopping again, no worries. We aren't going to starve.

b u l k   f o o d

I purchase things like flour, sugar, dried fruit, nuts, seeds, and chocolate (mmm, chocolate) from a bulk food store. Since the bulk food store is at a distance, I only shop there when I'm already in the neighborhood. I bring those items home and fill my kitchen containers (wide-mouth Ball canning jars), store the rest in a bin under the cabinet. I keep dried fruit and seeds on hand to eat when I'd rather work than cook. Buying these items in bulk means I use much less packaging, which makes my inner tree-hugging, zero-waste child very happy. Plus, the prices are great!

If you have space, try building a shallow set of shelves to fit wide mouth Ball canning jars. You'll have your food neatly stored right at hand. If you move your tiny house from time to time, you might consider adding a little wooden rail or two brads holding a wire to the shelf to keep kamikaze jars in place when the house is in motion. Also, every time you plan to move your home, stop shopping for a while before the move and eat whatever is on hand to clear out the extra weight. I will sometimes pack a few boxes of heavier things in the car when we are moving the house, just to lighten the load. It can't hurt. In addition to the many ways a washcloth is useful for cleaning one's person or one's home, they are also ideal packing material when you're going to drive your house "over the river and through the woods" or across the country.

o n - l i n e
I keep a nice selection of spices, specialty smoked sea salt, and peppercorns on hand and I buy them on-line in bulk from Atlantic Spice Company. I have a collection of essential oils that can be used in a smoothie, or in buttercream icing on a cake, or baked into cakes and cookies, or added with olive oil to hot pasta or cold pasta salad. I also purchase these on-line with a whole-sale membership from Young Living. Essential oils are space saving, they have health benefits, they don't go bad, and they are remarkably flavorful, so it's a win-win!

herbs, spices & essential oils
https://tinyhousefoodie.com/2018/01/22/16-herbs-spices-and-essential-oils/

e g g s
I go out of my way to buy farm-fresh eggs from a market near me where I know they come from local farmers who are growing happy yada-yada chickens who are laying yada-yada eggs. I call them yada-yada eggs because it amuses me that we have to add "free range, vegetarian fed, cage free" and other such labels to something like eggs. We should be able to call these yada yada eggs just "eggs" and the rest of them should be the ones wearing lengthy strings of labels. We've got things a little turned around these days.

When we had the restaurant, we learned that

eggs can legally be held at the farm for up to 30 days, and they can be at the market for another 30 days, and still be considered "fresh". That does not even count how long they sit in the home fridge before someone decides to use them. Just the idea of eating an egg that is already two months old is enough to turn me off the very idea of an omelet. That's why I buy eggs from local farmers where I know they are fresh and, as a bonus, we can return the egg cartons and they will be used again and again. And seeing those egg cartons recycled makes me happy.

Better yet, our area has recently approved a backyard chicken law, so it is now legal to keep a few hens in the back yard. As far as I'm concerned, an egg fresh from the hen is one of nature's wonders. And that way, what you feed them and how you handle the fresh eggs is up to you. That, in my mind, is the very definition of freedom and freshness. And there are so many amazing things that can be made from these beautiful little marvels! Chief among them is the super simple, never out-of-style, chef's favorite: the omelet.

f i s h

I have found two great sources in my area to buy wild-caught fish. I used to have a neighbor who went fishing early in the morning and he'd bring me a small cooler of a dozen fresh trout packed in snow, caught just that morning. That was delightful, but unfortunately I don't have a neighbor like that anymore.

These days we enjoy shopping at our favorite international grocery store. The staff in the fresh fish department will scale the fish and cut steaks for us, and they even make recommendations on the best way to cook the various kinds of fish. We've tried all sorts of fish, and even an octopus, as a result of having a great fish market not-too-far from us. All the mess happens at the market, no need for any of that to come home to the tiny house. When you get the fish home, you can move right to the fun part of preparing a feast for your family. To minimize fishy smells, choose the freshest fish, and steam it or bake it in parchment. When the meal is over, remove the remainder of the fish and the packaging from your house.

chapter 18
the pantry

How do you stock a tiny house pantry? Here is a strategy to get you started: make three lists. From these lists you can choose the ingredients to purchase for the week.

snacks and starters

First, make a list of snacks and starters that you can eat when rushed for time that will tide you over until a meal is ready. In a pinch, these can serve as meals, so make sure they're healthy. Items in this category help to keep us from picking up poor-quality convenience foods on the fly. I especially enjoy healthy snacks such as almonds, apples, and avocados, and when I'm at the bulk food store I stock up on the ingredients for trail mix. I like to keep a jar of my favorite salsa on hand and pair it with those bowl-shaped tortillas. We also enjoy hummus and carrots. My Austrian is always happy with a lovely cheese and a loaf of crusty bread. From this list, I choose two or three starters or snack options for the week and shop accordingly.

sweets

Second, if you have a sweet tooth like I do, make a list of treats that can be made in small portions that you can enjoy when you just want a bite of something sweet and lovely to finish a meal. Go for small quantities of something high-quality rather than the other way around. When I know the week will be especially busy, I choose a good-quality gourmet candy bar to eat that week. If I think I will have a bit more time, I'll choose a simple recipe for a sweet treat to make early in the week and enjoy all week long. This keeps me snacking on better-quality sweets that are more satisfying than low-quality sweets, and that way I eat less. Keep this simple, though; there is no point having complex recipes and intentions without the time to follow through. You don't want your food storage area to become a source of frustration, so keep it simple and minimize ingredients. A very nice dark chocolatebarmightbejustthething(Iprefercacaocontentof between 50% and 60%), and my Austrian was weaned on milk chocolate, yum!

m e a l s
Finally, make a list of your favorite meals based on the produce that is currently in season. You can find a list of what produce is in season by searching your state's agricultural website for a chart. Right now I have lots of tomatoes and basil in the garden, so we are making BLT's (with basil instead of lettuce), Caprese salad, and homemade pizza. A super simple meal is "pasta" made with spiral-sliced zucchini instead of noodles, and topped with garlic, onions, tomato, and basil (or your favorite Salsa Puttanesca recipe). It's fast and easy to make, and very satisfying. I also enjoy a lovely omelet for breakfast with fresh yada yada eggs and vegetables and herbs I picked from the garden that morning. From this list of favorite, simple, and seasonal meals you can create a shopping list for your visit to the market.

I like to have a balance of meals that can be made by just one of us pretty quickly, and meals that are more of a celebration where we would be cooking together. It is also nice to have a comfort-food option on hand, like shrimp and grits. Sometimes we'll be hungry for something specific, so we'll choose those ingredients. At other times one or the other of us will simply make something up based on what is in the house at the moment, it's a surprise.

It is great to sit down and plan this out on paper and make a list, which saves time in the store. I must confess that I actually do this on the fly in the market, and since it's just the two of us and our little dog, this isn't difficult. I check the produce and see what is available and looking especially nice this week, and shop accordingly. I will also check the meat counter and look for a nice wild-caught fish that would make a special meal for us for the week. Based on what I find there, I make a menu for the week in my head and that guides my shopping.

It is always a challenge for me not to over-buy. I love fresh produce. It's my favorite part of any market and always my favorite thing on the plate. It is easy to see beautiful produce and go overboard with shopping. So plan your food choices around what is fresh and lovely, and keep the quantities in check. Choose the most colorful vegetables and fruits, and choose different items each week: variety replaces quantity. Choose fresh fruits and vegetables rather than canned. We do not miss at all having a battery of cans clogging up our valuable pantry space.

You can stock a tiny house pantry by choosing healthy snacks and starters that will keep you away from poor-quality convenience foods (and their excessive packaging) when you are tired and pressed for time. Shopping for a few high-quality sweet treats will be more satisfying than a larger quantity of a low-quality item. Finally, choosing meals around the beautiful fresh produce that is available will keep you eating fresh, whole food that is healthy and satisfying. Having a range of quick and easy meals along with more special meal options will make sharing a meal the highlight of the day.

right-sizing the pantry
https://tinyhousefoodie.com/2018/01/19/tackle-the-pantry-day-15/

chapter 19
less buy, more DIY

If you built your tiny haven home with your own hands, you are already a Do-It-Yourselfer. It's no stretch to apply that same approach to making food. Even if you purchased your tiny haven-home ready-made, you were still drawn in by a movement of creative homes made by creative people. When we apply that same creative spirit to the way we eat, we're not just enjoying better quality spaces, we're also enjoying better quality food. Instead of buying expensive (or cheap) prepared food, or going out to eat often, we can make the food ourselves. We can explore the many variations on a theme provided by a recipe, and even save some money in the process. And if the food we enjoy happens to look good on Facebook or Instagram, that's a plus—but it's not the goal. Living a simple, purposeful life is the goal, and that may not always look like the photos on Pinterest. It is, nevertheless, a worthy goal.

Often the main difference between a chef and a home cook (besides having a full staff and a much larger budget) is that a chef makes everything from scratch. A home cook buys stock, a chef makes it. A home cook buys mayo, a chef makes it. Cooking like a chef may mean buying less and doing a lot more DIY, and often that isn't about space, it's about quality. As a tiny house foodie, this is where you get to choose your sweet spot on the spectrum of DIY cooking. You can catch a live animal, dispatch it, dress it out, cook it, and serve it. You can render the fat to make lard, and make your own soap. You can save the bones and make stock that can be used in all sorts of recipes.

You may choose to go vegetarian or vegan as well. Helen and Scott Nearing (Authors of *The Good Life:*

Helen and Scott Nearing's Sixty Years of Self-Sufficient Living) were pacifists who would not do violence to any person or beast. "I became a vegetarian because I was persuaded that life is as valid for other creatures as it is for humans. I do not need dead animal bodies to keep me alive, strong and healthy. Therefore, I will not kill for food" (from *The Making of a Radical* by Scott Nearing). I have noticed that there are quite a few vegetarians and vegans in the tiny house community. Refrigeration and food storage is much simpler without the hazards of time and temperature that come with raw proteins. And while I'm not a vegetarian or vegan, I do respect this approach. I prefer a diet that uses meat for flavor or as a side rather than the main event.

There are many other DIY food options. You can forage for berries and make your own jam. You can make your own cheese. You can learn all about edible plants and turn some "weeds" into salad. You can grow your own wheat and thresh it, grind the kernels into flour, and make your own bread. You can make your own apple cider vinegar, and there are lots of lovely things to ferment and pickle. There are all sorts of ways you can get in touch with your food, develop some useful skills, and create better, healthier options for yourself and your family. Plus, learning all those different things is really fun! The opportunities for creativity are truly endless.

I don't like processed food, but I don't make everything from scratch, either. I'm somewhere in the middle, and I bet you are also. I love to make my own vegetable stock or bone broth. I love making my own food from good ingredients. That way I can avoid toxic ingredients and enjoy a much better flavor. Xaver makes home-made bread each Tuesday and donates some to a cause he values. I have tried various kinds of fermenting, including country wine and apple cider vinegar. I have made a lot of yogurt and even some kinds of cheese. I enjoy learning how to make things, and I find the exploration and learning invigorating. I am making an investment in the quality of my food and I know what I'm eating, plus I'm sending a lot less packaging to the landfill and that matters to me also. You don't have to make everything from scratch. Just pick your favorites to DIY so that you eat better, avoid toxins more effectively, and improve your quality of life and wellness. And the sense of accomplishment that comes with making real honest food with your own hands is one of the things that makes this DIY tiny life so rewarding. If you can live this tiny DIY lifestyle, you can explore DIY food as well! Pull out your favorite recipe, make a grocery list, and get started.

chapter 20
cleaning

the great kitchen clean out

Sometimes I just take a break from shopping and we eat up whatever is hanging around, and only when we've cleaned out the place pretty well do I head back to the store again. It's amazing how much food hangs out along the edges of a kitchen if you're not purposeful about cleaning it out now and then. Clean out the freezer and eat the mystery meat that you find in the back corner or cook it up for the dog. Clean out the fridge and compost anything that looks like it has met its maker. Get rid of anything growing felty pads. Just keep nibbling away until you've cleaned out the kitchen, then scoot off to the store again.

At one time I lived in the boonies and shopping was a real production because the nearest grocery store was an hour away. Living that far out can lead you to develop habits that are counter-productive to life in a tiny house. If you know it could be a while before you get back to the grocery, you'll purchase less fresh food and more shelf staples (highly processed foods). You may also tend to over-buy in case a snow storm comes and you can't get out for a few extra days. All of that was fine when I had the storage space but these days I keep less food on hand.

Like everything else about living tiny, shopping and food storage involves your mindset. Learning what works in your situation may take some trial and error. Joyful adaptability is one of the greatest gifts we give ourselves. We learn from our situation, make needed changes, and transition to living a new way because that's what it takes to grow into our new normal.

clean as you cook

One of the skills that a chef learns early on is to always clean as you cook. A cleaning cloth is part of the uniform, so to speak. Spills are cleaned up immediately and anything dropped on the floor is instantly picked up. Broken dishes are always removed quickly. (Don't believe everything you see on TV about how professional kitchens work.) There is never a time when a professional leaves a mess in the kitchen as they work. During my career in professional kitchens, I almost always worked with people who kept their space clean as a whistle— there were very few exceptions. Of course those exceptions make great stories, but nobody wants to eat food that comes from those kitchens.

In a tiny house, there is no such thing as a little mess. If you don't already have the habit of immediately cleaning up every kitchen mess you make, it's time to develop this habit. Nothing makes a tiny house feel close and squalid like a mess. A meal isn't complete until the kitchen is clean. That way you are always eating your meal in a clean kitchen, and when that is the case, cooking is a delight.

cleaning a tiny house

> "Cleaning house is not my life's work."
> —me

One of my favorite aspects of living tiny is how quick and easy it is to clean my small space. No need for a loud vacuum, I just use a broom. It's hand-made by one of my artist friends, but it is a broom. No need for special gear, a washcloth is all I need. I have found cleaning in a tiny house to be surprisingly fun. I can have my home clean by 10 a.m., I can have it clean-clean by noon, and I can have it Mennonite-clean by 3 p.m. And this is very rewarding. Cleaning house is not my life purpose, and since I live in a tiny house, it doesn't have to be.

cleaning supplies

I'm able to skip the cleaning supply aisle in the grocery store because I make my own cleaning potions. I didn't just throw them all out and start over with natural non-toxic alternatives. I simply used up what I had on hand, and when I ran out of something I did the research and made my own non-toxic alternative. For more information about this, along with lots of great recipes, see my book *Mennonite Clean: Pure & Simple Recipes for the Green Clean Home*.

paper products

I also skip the paper product aisle when shopping because I have a stash of cloth alternatives. It makes me so happy that I no longer need to find space in my tiny house for rolls of paper towels (those things are space hogs!). I don't even need to stash a neat stack of tissue boxes on the floor of my closet. It's just not needed. I use handkerchiefs for napkins, paper towels, and tissues. I use washcloths for cleaning. I didn't make this transition overnight by any means, but I really love not buying paper products, I love that I don't have to find room for them in my house, or in my waste stream! More information about this is also available in my upcoming book *Mennonite Clean: Pure & Simple Recipes for the Green Clean Home*.

detoxing your clean
https://tinyhousefoodie.com/2018/01/03/day-3-right-sizing-your-kitchen-in-2018/

chapter 21
taming trash

One of the things you learn pretty quickly when you live in 125 square feet is how much space is required for ordinary trash. We quickly realized that we didn't want a trash can taking up valuable real estate in the house, and we didn't want to be storing bulky disposables that would turn into bulky trash. We began transitioning to a greener and more environmentally-friendly approach and it solved a very immediate trash problem for us. For example, a roll of paper towels takes up a lot of space to store when it's new, especially if you find them on sale and buy several rolls at a time. I used to stuff rolls of paper towels in some pretty weird places in my home. But once you give up a lot of closet real estate to go tiny, you may find that you don't want to give up even more space to the likes of a roll of paper towels. One of the first things the downsizing pros recommend is to keep only items that serve numerous purposes. That includes disposables that are one use away from the landfill. It's rewarding to go zero-waste as an environmental choice, but also because it saves so much space.

I purchased four dozen 100% cotton handker-chiefs (which are inexpensive when bought in packs of one dozen) from Dharma Trading Company and I dyed them in my favorite colors. (I never iron them!) At first I used them to replace tissues and saved myself the cost and the space needed for storing tissue boxes. I was inspired by how successful that was, and it didn't cause an overload of laundry like I feared. Soon I was using my fun handkerchiefs for cloth napkins as well. I quick-ly found that the cloth alternatives were much softer and suited me better and I continued replacing paper products in my home with cloth options.

When I was dating my handsome husband, I loved ginger ale and usually had a plastic bottle with me. That's fine when you have a 3,000-square-foot kitchen or work in a spacious office. When you transition to a tiny house, suddenly two or three of those plastic bottles are incredibly invasive space hogs, and I quickly resented having to deal with them. I started drinking water with lemon or tea (even ginger tea) instead. It was no sacrifice to keep those big plastic bottles out of my house because it made the space much more usable.

That got me thinking and doing a little research. Soon I was inspired by the Zero Waste movement. The more I read and the more I tried out alternatives to single-use products, the more I found those approaches really suited my tiny life. My tiny house brought me closer to nature. Living a greener life was a lovely side effect of finding more creative ways to live comfortably in my tiny space. I would not have expected that to be one of the life transformations of going tiny, but there you have it. Going green makes living in a tiny house more satisfying—not just from an environmental perspective, but from a space saving perspective as well. Believe me, when you live in 125 square feet and it starts to fill up with bulky disposables and trash, change is inevitable. Pay attention to what feels irritating in your small space, make incremental changes to address those challenges. There are a lot of surprising little details about living tiny, and you'll soon find the simple solutions that work best for you. There is nothing about living tiny to fear; just stay adaptable and creative and you'll be fine.

taming trash
https://tinyhousefoodie.com/2018/01/05/day-5-right-sizing-your-kitchen/

part 4

garden
fresh

chapter 22
freshness

Freshness is the single most important element in creating great food. It's the key difference between a good dish and a spectacular dish. A home cook with a garden has an advantage over a professional chef when they can pick something in the garden and immediately prepare a meal with it. There is no fresher food, there is no better food. I have a number of kale plants in containers outside my home and I have been enjoying fresh kale right off the plant as part of my breakfast omelet. Buying kale in the store is hit or miss, as it may already be wilted and sad looking by the time you see it in the grocery, and by the time you've gotten it home it may have already given up the ghost. This is why I grow a few containers of kale. Freshness is the key to great food, and that has nothing to do with the size of your kitchen. A tiny kitchen is no handicap when it comes to great ingredients.

A friend of mine had a sweet corn farm and we joked that you put a pot of water on to boil, went to pick the corn, and by the time the water boiled, the corn was shucked and ready to steam. Everyone who helped shuck and silk the corn was right there and ready to eat when the corn came off the heat. There is no better way to eat sweet corn. You can still serve it with fresh pesto, or smoked paprika butter, or even just brown butter and pink Himalayan sea salt. You can still do your own gourmet twist on freshly steamed sweet corn, but freshness is the key. Fresh sweet corn is sweet like candy and it is divine. Sweet corn from the grocery has already been picked for days, and it's starchy and gummy. It may not even be worth the trouble to shuck and silk it. Potatoes are similar. Freshly dug tiny little new potatoes are sweet rather than starchy, and when cooked with olive oil and herbs and eaten right away, there is nothing better. A garden is a culinary advantage. Having a small kitchen won't keep you from growing or finding great ingredients with which to cook.

homesteading

Some folks grow great big gardens and preserve the food through canning, fermenting, freezing, and dehydration so that they can eat their garden produce all year long. These preparation processes take space. The equipment required for canning, dehydrating, and freezing may make it difficult to do in a tiny home, although I know folks who have done so. Even if living tiny and homesteading is not your thing, you can still enjoy growing a selection of fresh herbs, fruits, and vegetables in your garden. There is a lot of middle ground between growing a few herbs and growing a garden designed to feed your family all year. So wherever you are or want to be on that continuum, you can make it happen.

No matter how much or how little you grow, food you've grown yourself comes with a sense of accomplishment that is good for the soul. That is just as nourishing as the nutritional value. And when times get bad and the economic system experiences some challenges, growing your own food is a way to insulate yourself from drama and volatility on the world stage. Whatever you do, try to grow something because freshness is one of the keys to creating great healthy food, plus it saves you money at the market.

container garden

To get started, grow a few pots of herbs and maybe an heirloom cherry tomato plant. Home-grown tomatoes are so much better than store-purchased tomatoes that they shouldn't even share the same name!

moving a container garden

When we move our tiny house, we put the container garden in the pickup truck and just take them with us and find a new sunny spot for them at the new parking place. I have also brought some plants inside and put them in the kitchen sink with a few things wedged in around them in the sink to keep them secure. We move the tiny garden inside the tiny house, and haven't had any problems doing so.

I haven't tried to grow even a small garden when I knew we were going to be parked in one sport for a very short season. Furthermore, I'm not big on spending my morning outside in the heat finding and scraping squash bug eggs from the back of the leaves on my squash plants, so these days I often buy more squash than I grow. I think the key here is finding the balance of what works for you. There is no wrong way to go about this. If you're comfortable growing basil, but are fine purchasing the rest, that's great.

growing a garden

I grew up in a Mennonite farmhouse on a cattle farm. We had a large garden and a root cellar where we kept neat rows of fruits and vegetables we canned (along with a few resident spiders). I remember two huge chest freezers in the basement that were always full with vegetables and fruits from the garden, as well as beef from the farm. The farm was very nearly self-sufficient with meat production, a large garden, and fruit trees, plus there was enough beef to sell what we didn't use.

There was also a lot of work involved, and I have many memories of canning peaches and making applesauce with my grandmother, my mom, and my aunts. When we put together a meal, there would be beef the men raised along with greens and fruits that the women preserved from the garden. It all came with the reminder that we'd worked together to bring it to the table, and it also came with a sense of community—a sense of being part of a group working toward a common goal. We could also look around the freezer or neat rows of canned fruit and veggies and appreciate the visible results of a job well done.

I think we miss this with the way we do food in our modern world. We've made food faster, but we haven't made it better. All those rows and rows of prepared food in the grocery store, all the gadgets and pricey gear doesn't make the food better. And when we miss the opportunity to actually cook with a good knife on a solid cutting board to create an honest meal, we also miss the nourishment of soul and spirit that is found in this simple work. Cooking is a love language, and mastering the basics of good knife work and choosing great fresh ingredients and preparing them with mindful presence is the way to make beautiful food that is satisfying and nourishing to the spirit, soul, and body. And that is one of the elements of tiny house cooking that I really love.

chapter 23
tiny house foodie garden

Many of us who live in tiny houses are not going to go much beyond some container gardening. However, if you should decide to give it a whirl, I have a recommendation.

I was recently able to expand beyond my container garden into an actual tiny garden. I'm loving it! I did a bit of quick research on straw bale gardening and the lasagna gardening method, and got started. I combined the concepts of the straw bale garden with the lasagna garden concept by putting six straw bales in a rectangle and composting in the open space in the middle in the style of a lasagna garden. I have lots of vegetables and herbs planted in the bales, and those plants are doing great. I enjoyed fresh kale, Swiss chard, and herbs from this garden all summer. We planted a few extra straw bales with tomatoes, peppers, squash, and melons, and those are doing surprisingly well also. What a pleasure to pick something and bring it inside and make a meal. Having great, fresh produce so close at hand has been a real pleasure!

My Austrian gathered those bales for me, and we positioned them on top of cardboard. I watered them with organic liquid fertilizer to speed their decomposition and left them alone for a few weeks. I planted some seeds in pots by our back step, and when they were happy, hardy seedlings and big enough to move, I transplanted them to the straw bales. This is an interesting process that involves digging a clump of straw out of the wet bale to make room for soil, mixing organic soil with some good quality organic fertilizer and filling the hole with the plant and soil mixture, carefully covering that dirt with a bit of straw to retain moisture.

This turned out to be remarkably effective, and since the plants quickly grow into that soil and maybe beyond into the straw bale, it's a good idea to continue to add a good quality organic fertilizer specific to the needs of the herbs or vegetables you plant there.

Lasagna gardening is an insanely easy no-dig, no-till organic gardening method that yields great garden soil. To try lasagna gardening, simply layer brown material such as leaves, shredded paper, and sawdust with green layers such as vegetable scraps and lawn trimmings. There is no need to be exact about it, just pile things in together. Over the course of the year, the layers of compost decompose into a raised garden bed the following season. The brilliance of this method (which is not at all original to me) is that you can have a lovely organic garden without turning a single spade full of dirt. This combination of straw bale gardening with lasagna garden composting was a great way for us to put together a compost pile in a way that isn't objection-able to our neighbors and didn't require investing in a lot of gear. Another plus is that if we end up staying here for a number of seasons, we will get to enjoy the compost.

Our neighbor was in the process of removing a water feature with a lot of rocks when we moved the bales into place. He gave us all the stones we could carry, so we used them to build a little makeshift stone wall around our Tiny House Garden, which makes it look nice and may also help warm the soil and extend the growing season.

I could imagine continuing to garden this spot and adding new Tiny House Foodie gardens over time, if we were going to be here long. I suppose we'll see. I think this may be the easiest gardening I've ever done. I didn't have to get a shovel or turn a single bit of soil, I just put everything in place and nature does what nature does. I consider this the ideal tiny house garden and compost for my needs and it has been ridiculously easy.

chapter 24
cooking as meditation

"I'm just someone who likes cooking
and for whom sharing food
is a form of expression."
—Maya Angelou

For me, cooking without lots of gear has become an act of meditation and a way to focus my energy. Instead of pulling out a loud appliance, I relish the quiet knife work of cutting herbs and vegetables by hand. It doesn't really take longer to do, and you get to have your hands in the food, enjoy the colors and textures, and make your mark. Plus, cleaning up is so much simpler. We can take the time to cook in a way that produces simple, honorable food, food that says "I love you, and that's why I'm making something special." Cooking is the ultimate self-care in that it recognizes our value as individuals, made in the image of God, and therefore worth treating with respect and care. Mindful preparation of food with a mind kept firmly in the present moment to savor each element of food preparation is a way of embracing purposeful simplicity and sharing love. Preparing a meal in my tiny house has focused that idea of cooking with love in a way that cooking in my grand restaurant never did for me. I blame my epiphanies about creating great food on going tiny. It's been a remarkable change of mindset for me.

You can focus on not having space and fall into the poverty mindset, or you can focus on embracing purposeful simplicity. The more you focus on embracing simplicity, the more you'll find that it embraces you and makes you free. As we embrace simplicity, living tiny becomes less of a means to an end, and more of a life-style of liberty.

eating together

In a tiny house, having a place to sit together and eat is more important than storage space for food. We've found that a table of 24 x 30 inches is perfect for two, and it can be stretched to an intimate gathering of five. We also like that our banquette seating doubles as our living room sofa. Four can eat together in cozy comfort in this space, five with the addition of a folding chair.

Inviting someone into your haven-home to share a meal is an amazing act of vulnerability, hospitality, and connection in a world that is anything but. We savor these opportunities when they surface. We put aside our devices and enjoy food and conversation. This simple-but-revolutionary act is a beautiful thing in a world of screens. These intimate moments are exactly the reason we considered going tiny to begin with. These intimate moments are the reason we continue living tiny when the novelty has faded and the tires show some wear. We choose intimate spaces. We choose real connections. We choose purpose. We choose liberty.

chapter 25
creating sacred space

There have been a number of times over our years of living tiny that Xaver and I have faced some really crazy schnitzel together. In those times, it's really easy to think, "Poor Me" (with emphasis on the POOR) and look around and focus on the tiny space and the lack of this or that and let it all become about poverty rather than about simplicity and proactive life choices. Let me tell you, that is deeply unpleasant.

We are trained to think that having a lot of stuff equals wealth. Dominant culture tells us that a homeless guy is worthless. A man with a nice house, nice yard, and a couple cars is a pretty good guy. The man with four houses, an expensive collection of cars, and a business empire is really something special. Billionaires are gods. This is the perception of dominant culture, but is it true? Of course not. We're seeing day-by-day proof in our political arena that this is not at all true.

Xaver and I chose to be houseless, not homeless. Or perhaps it's a sort of intentional homelessness, at least in the house-on-a-foundation sense, but that doesn't mean we are poor. When we lose sight of that, we have to go back and remind ourselves of the truth.

We've had some battles that brought us back together at the end of the day feeling like the world had beaten us up and spit us out. Telling each other what happened is one thing, stewing on hurt feelings, anger, and bitter disappointment is another thing. Combine that heaviness with the reality of a small space, and it can start to feel crushing. Sometimes we have gone outside to brush off the negativity, talk, and share some sarcasm until we've reached the laughter, and then scoot back inside and enjoy our evening. At times we wash the cares of the day off by washing our hands at the sink. Sometimes I will whisk the burdens off his shoulders with my hands, as if worries were something like dandruff that can just be swept away (they can be) and he will do the same for me. We agree together that heaviness is not allowed in our tiny space. There simply isn't room. And in that way, living tiny is turned from a negative into a positive. When I'm tempted to feel poor and wretched, I remind myself that there isn't space for negativity in my home.

Sometimes, something horrible, stupid, or devastating is happening in the world and from the sound of the people on the news, the sky is falling. The end is nigh. No. Turn off the TV. Put on some nice music and play a game of cards instead. Light a beeswax candle. Say a prayer. Say to the big, bad, crazy world: "No, none of that schnitzel in here, thank you very much!" (And mean it!) Our home is a sanctuary. We really can unplug, turn off, or change the channel away from the world's noise. Ah, peace. It's glorious.

Sometimes we turn the lights down low, put a fire in the fireplace (which is what we call lighting a beeswax candle in a glass), pour ourselves a drink, put on some nice music, and play cards. We use the excuse of our tiny space to encourage each other to keep the peace within its walls, and push the dreadful things outside. When we leave for work in the morning, we can face those things. But on the inside, this space is about peace, tranquility, and love. Whatever it is, it can wait till morning when we go off to work and can deal with it. This space is our sacred haven. No trespassing.

It helps. Try it. For some reason, the fact that the space is small and cozy really does focus the connection of intimacy. It really is possible to use the tender walls of a tiny home to create space that is sacred and healing.

part 5

tiny
haven
home

chapter 26
entertaining

the tiny house exemption

Sometimes, having a tiny house can be used to liberate you from some pesky expectations. "I'm sorry, I know you'd like for me to host Thanksgiving this year. However, I live in a tiny house and there wouldn't be room." How often have you wanted to have an exemption that could be trotted out in situations like this? In fact, using the size of your home as an excuse to get out of situations that would make you miserable is a great perk of living tiny. The truth is, large homes may have a combination of private and public spaces, therefore having guests is only somewhat invasive. In a tiny home, the entire home is private space, every last square inch. Even the porch. Maybe even the well-worn path to your front door.

For an introvert like myself, having someone in that private space may feel like an invasion. Even if the invasion is a neighbor with a basket of your favorite cookies still warm from the oven, it may still feel like an invasion. This is when your tiny home becomes a shield and you simply say a polite "No, thank you" to whatever invasion is being cooked up by saying "I'm sorry, I live in a tiny house and there just wouldn't be room." Try not to say it with a huge grin. You might not want to let your relief show. Be polite, but firm. Try saying, "We might be more comfortable meeting in a more spacious location." Keep in mind that you determine what is "enough" space for your home. Not someone else. If you determine there would not be enough space, there isn't. Period. It's the tiny house exemption, and it is wonderful.

Where my home is currently parked, if you knock

on my front door, you've already passed through what I consider to be private space long before you were on my front porch raising your hand to knock. If you made it that far without my little dog alerting me of your presence, my dog is about to get very loud while we all deal with the surprise of having you right there all up in my grill.

My home is currently parked in a grove of walnut trees away from the road, completely out of sight for three seasons of the year. That is a purposeful choice. While my husband is the most extroverted of extroverts, I am not. I am a writer with ADD, and distractions are a real challenge for me in my work. Having the forest noises and animals around me is enough to keep me distracted by the ever-fascinating parade of wildlife near my home. I'm not interested in giving tours or hosting impromptu discussions of all things tiny house in the middle of my work day. I have zero interest in answering questions about composting toilets. I'm also not really an activist working to raise the visibility of tiny house living. I have work that matters and I want to get on with it.

Of course there are exceptions when it's time to gather some very special folks into the intimate embrace of the tiny home. In those times, inviting someone to join you for a meal is an act of hospitality that is intimate and loving.

words matter

"My house is too small for that." The truth is, if you live in a tiny house and you want to do something, you'll find a way. Do yourself and all of us tiny house folks a favor: Don't say your house is too small. It isn't. Choose different words, because words matter. You may say it knowing it's not really true, but there you are listening to yourself lie. Don't. If your house really is too small for things that are important to you, build an annex, rent additional space, or move. Create the life and space you need to breathe free.

It may seem an insignificant point, but how you

speak about your home matters. "My house is too small" may be a similar idea to "There wouldn't be room," but "My house is too small" is a derogatory judgment that your haven-home is "too" something-or-other. As any gentlemen can tell you, such remarks are no compliment. "I don't have space" is a statement of lack, "I don't have..." Living in a tiny house is not about poverty, it's about simplicity, therefore saying "I don't have..." is a misrepresentation of your situation. Not only are you telling someone else of your lack, you are also reminding yourself. Our culture constantly reminds us that there is never a lack of lack; the main goal of billions of dollars of marketing aimed at each of us is to teach us what we lack and create a sense of need.

Gratitude reminds us that we are rich in many things, especially love. We are therefore free of the need to impress, prove our worth in a financial sense, prove ourselves, or consume for the sake of consuming. Focus matters, words matter. Finally, saying "There wouldn't be room" may be a simple way to express the fact that, in some cases, the invasion of private space isn't appealing. It's perfectly acceptable to be honest.

Living tiny is supposed to be about right-sizing your life. If you don't particularly care to host guests in your home, size your home accordingly. The tiny house is your friend on this front. You can tell the truth about your situation and mention that there may be more comfortable options like restaurants or public parks, but don't make it about your lack and don't disrespect your haven-home. If you want others to be respectful of your choice to go tiny, your own language should also be respectful of your choice.

chapter 27
tiny hospitality

"Dining with one's friends and beloved family
is certainly one of life's primal
and most innocent delights,
one that is both soul-satisfying and eternal."
—Julia Child

There are a number of very special people that I enjoy having in my tiny haven-home. We have a small table that we can eat around, and inviting someone into our haven-home and sharing hospitality is a purposeful and caring choice. The intimacy of small spaces may turn your conversation far deeper than an ordinary space would. (I'm making the assumption that you have a table that folks can gather around rather than the ubiquitous sofa aimed at a television.) Coming together around a table will bring you a sense of connection and intimacy. Welcoming someone into your haven-home and sharing great food is a way of communicating to someone that they really matter. No matter what I've said about the invasion of people on my tiny house space, I still love to have very special people in my home and cook for them. Tiny homes are built to bring people closer to the things and people that matter.

In fact, entertaining in your tiny home gives your guests the opportunity to learn how you live. It may even give them permission to look outside of dominant culture's way of living. After all, when folks experience hospitality that is more concerned with connection than production, it liberates friends to do the same. Guests actually relax when they realize you are making them a part of the family rather than putting on a show for them.

hosting a party

How do you go about celebrating with the people you appreciate most? Food! How about Thanksgiving? (Go big or go home?) The biggest food holiday of the calendar year is Thanksgiving and this is the holiday that tests the seams of even conventional kitchens. So how do you make the full Thanksgiving feast without having to also move out of your own house to make room? I got so carried away writing on this topic that I decided to add another book to the Tiny House Foodie series: *Simple Generosity: Entertaining in a Tiny House.*

a tiny thanksgiving

I suppose it depends on your expectations for a holiday. For years I hosted the "Anti-Thanksgiving" meal at for folks who were away from their loved ones on that day. I wasn't anti-gratitude, just anti boring Thanksgiving food. I'd make pizza and French silk pie, or maybe tacos and a dulce-de-leche cake. I've never been a great fan of turkey as a culinary statement, so I'd build a menu around the foods we preferred. After all, a celebration of Thanksgiving is possible with any menu.

One year my home was full of international girls who had never had a traditional American Thanksgiving meal. That year I pulled out all the stops and made the traditional meal, and it was great. I also had an obscenely huge kitchen at the time, so there were no limitations and no need for any special space-conscious creativity.

Decide what you want the menu to be, then start planning ahead. Instead of mashed potatoes that must be done at the last moment, make them ahead of time and put them in a baking dish with garlic, Panko, and sea salt on top. Or make potato gratin the day before and bake it the day of. Or include your potatoes in the roasting pan with the meat. Plan to make a maximum of three menu items and invite your guests to also bring a dish to share or fill in with items that can be purchased locally. Keep it simple, go for quality rather than quantity.

chapter 28
conclusion

After Xaver and I got out of the restaurant ownership rat race, and we decided to go tiny, new dreams were materializing where the restaurant dream had been. I wanted land where I could grow a garden and where we could build a modest but interesting home on a foundation. I also wanted to take some time to finish one of my books and see if a publisher would be interested. Living tiny was a means to an end for us. At least, that's how it started.

Surprisingly, living tiny started to change me. When we went tiny, I designed a 1,200 square foot "dream house." After six months of living tiny, I took up my pencil again and designed a 900 square foot dream house. A year later I was designing an even smaller one. Along the way we were realizing that living tiny agreed with us. The dream was changing. We still wanted to find land and build a house, but not 1,200 square feet. Maybe not 125 square feet with no loft like we currently have, just a slightly more relaxed version of our current space with the special luxuries of a lovely bath tub, a masonry heater (like the Kachelofen my Austrian remembers from his youth), a laundry space, and a rather spacious closet. All that still adds up to a rather small house, and it sounds wonderful to me.

Living tiny also had some very palpable financial benefits for us. With no mortgage or rent payment, there was a difference in what was required each month. At first we didn't notice much change, but over time we realized that we had some breathing room financially. After a while, we saw our savings account grow. We took a Dave Ramsey class and read a book by Helen and Scott Nearing that inspired us to live debt free. In time we purchased a vintage Mercedes Benz we wanted (wanted, not needed) without a loan. Later on, we purchased another truck as well, and donated our old one. Those were the most stress-free auto purchases I'd ever experienced. I would highly recommend this life. Living tiny and staying out of debt has made a huge difference for us, and we are happy to recommend this life to anyone.

There were some other dreams as well. I have dreamed of being a published author for more than a decade and I already had a number of books partially written. Living tiny gave me the opportunity to take a creative writing class at Stanford, and to take some other classes with some of my favorite authors as well. It has given me a little extra time here and there to spend with super creative women who could teach me important skills. In time my dream of becoming a published author came into sight, and if you are holding this book in your hands, you already know how that turned out. Is living tiny really a sacrifice when it makes long-held hopes and dreams possible? I don't think so. Living tiny made it possible for me to see my dream of being a published author come true.

Living tiny has taught me gratitude. Gratitude is one of those secrets to a happy life that they don't teach you in school. Marketing convinces us that we need stuff, but living with gratitude teaches us to want less. It really is a game-changing attitude that is one of those little secrets to happiness. When I start to feel poor, I pull out the gratitude and tank up on the many blessings in my life! Gratitude changes everything!

Living tiny has enabled us to be more generous with ourselves and with others. Friends invited us to lunch so we joined them in their beautiful home for a lovely lunch. It's not that uncommon to take one's lunch hour to meet a friend, but in this case I glanced at the clock after the meal and it was nearing 4:00 pm, and we'd sat down at noon. We were having such a delight-ful time with our friends around a table of delicious food, we lost all track of time. Living tiny makes it possible to be generous with our time in other ways as well. My Austrian helps out in a variety of situations: car trouble, a downed tree, baking bread for a group that gathers for a meal each week. Living tiny allows him to be generous with his time. We have had some opportunities to be financially generous as well, and it has meant so much to be able to step in and quietly help out or meet a need here and there. I'll tell you, nothing else gives you a surge of energy and light like being present and able to help behind the scenes when a need arises. Generosity is absolutely invigorating and addictive, and having a taste of it will only make you want more. There is no more powerful antidote to materialism than generosity. Dominant culture teaches us to hoard and to grab and grasp everything we can. The truth is we are far happier when we're letting it go through our hands to people and causes that matter. In fact, when systems are in flux around us and important causes lose funding, we can step in and make a very real difference. You can't help if you're living right at the level of your income, but if you pay as you go and live on less than you make, you'll be able to really help out at times. And that matters! Generosity matters!

m e n n o n i t e

Sometimes I feel that I've been going tiny all my life. When I was a kid, I loved to play with shoe boxes and small colorful blocks. It was like an off-grid off-line version of Tetris, only I was designing tiny efficient houses inside my shoe boxes. That's where my second-hand Barbies lived.

In my community there was a message all over the place—bumper stickers, posters, shirts. It was "Live simply so that others may simply live" and it was every-where. That made an impression on me.

Growing up Mennonite may have predisposed me toward simplicity. Maybe there's just something in my blood as the granddaughter of a Mennonite Pas-tor. Then again, maybe there's just something that surfaces in anyone when you dare to step outside of conformity. Especially when odds aren't in your favor. Or maybe some of this is a reaction against hearing "But we have to have it!!" for the 20 years of my practice marriage—when I knew full well I could live without whatever-it-was.

Whatever the reasons, I loved the idea of going tiny. I read all the books, watched all the documentaries and daydreamed about building our own place. But once we took the leap, I found tiny house life pretty challenging. There were times when it was really frustrating to want space I didn't have. There were times I hated it. But we got creative. We found solutions. We adapted. I grew to love it, and love it fiercely. And now I don't want to ever go back to "normal" (whatever normal is).

og had an iron bed

When I was a kid, my parents took me to a campground conference that was a gathering of Mennonites from all over the region. All of us kids would play in the woods and the creek and go swimming during the day. In the evening as the sun set, the adults and children would all gather for an evening meal followed by community singing and a sermon. One night a gentlemen named Myron Augsberger preached. He was a tall, aristocratic man and a gifted speaker. I may have been about 9 years old or so, and somehow the way he spoke kept my full attention. He read us a passage from Deuteronomy about Og, king of Bashan. The text mentions that Og had an iron bed, in fact, that's all we know about him. The air was full of night noises, the fire was burning brightly, and the crowd had gathered in close. Paster Augsburger paced and preached!

Abraham believed God and it was credited to him as righteousness, but Og had an iron bed. Moses brought the family of Jacob out of slavery in Egypt and parted the Red Sea so that they walked through on dry ground. Og had an iron bed. Gideon led an army of 300 men into battle against the Midianites who had brought his community to the brink of starvation. They had so many soldiers that it was impossible to count them all, but Gideon and his small band of warriors won a great victory. Og had an iron bed. Esther went to her king and explained Haman's plot to kill all the Jews, and her people were saved. Og had an iron bed.

Paster Augsberger paced the floor and continued. Dr. Martin Luther King Jr. had a dream. "I have a dream that my four little children will one day live in a nation where they will not be judged by the color of their skin, but by the content of their character." (And not by the contents of their bank account.) King spoke that dream aloud and it was a transcendent moment. We heard him and his dream became our dream and it changed the course of a generation. Og had an iron bed.

Paster Augsberger told the stories of the heroes of the faith and contrasted each of them with Og and his iron bed. Og was the guy who got his name in the pages of a holy book only because of a thing he happened to own. That's it. I was just a child but I knew the difference in being known for owning some weird thing, as apposed to making a positive difference in the world.

another conference

I thought about Paster Augsberger's sermon again recently as I was preparing this manuscript. My parents invited me to another Mennonite conference. After the (phenomenal) singing and sermon there was a spread of international food prepared from recipes created by Mennonites around the world. My parents sat at the same table with Myron and Esther Augsberger. They've been friends for years and I was very happy to join them! When someone vacated the seat next to Myron, I took that seat and I told him about the sermon he preached all those years ago. He listened to me preach his sermon back to him. With a twinkle in his eye he said, "well, I have been known to preach on some pretty obscure passages." I told him "Well preachers don't preach on materialism anymore" and he instantly jumped in "That's right, they don't." He's moving a little slower these days, and his hair is completely white.

He's still one of the heroes of my faith.

I don't mind owning cool things, but it's not my life's purpose. It isn't difficult to see that there are a lot of honorable goals and dreams in life that are more interesting than owning some thing—even something as interesting as an iron bed. Or even... dare I say it... a tiny house. You don't have to be a person of faith, or even particularly spiritual to look around and note that there is more to life than stuff. When you get a little caught up in the stuff—even the tiny house stuff—remember Og and his iron bed.

We can go tiny, embrace simplicity, and still eat really well. You may not think that you can go tiny, but I know you can. God bless you. God bless your haven-home.

acknowledgments

Thank you to authors Ann Garvin, Ginger Moran, and Kerri Richardson who have encouraged my development as an author. Rachel Smith (who teaches creative writing at Stanford University) encouraged me to find and believe in my voice.

Tiny house authors Jay Shafer, Dee Williams, and Deek Diedrickson; off-grid homesteader and author Esther Emery; and the dynamic duo of Susan Schaefer Bernardo and Courtney Fletcher have each inspired me to embrace the adventure of the tiny life.

Patricia V. Davis, thank you for cheering me on, and for seeing my potential when I couldn't see it myself. I will always be in your debt.

To the team at H. D. Media Press, Inc., thank you for your encouragement throughout the publishing process. Word-smiths and visionaries like you make a writer shine and I'm so grateful for this amazing symbiosis! Mikki Soroczak, your editing work made this book so much better and I appreciate your careful and thoughtful approach so very much.

And last but not least, the love of my life, Xaver Wilhelmy. You keep reading me, refusing to see my flaws, and reminding me that I matter. This kind of love rocks my world. Thank you, Xaver, for believing in me, encouraging me to shine, and for creating a world where I can.

author bio

Carmen Shenk is a retired pastry chef/restaurant owner who has lived with her Austrian pipe organ builder and their cute cuddly dawg in 125 square feet since the fall of 2014. In 2018, they sold their tiny haven-home and began work on a Skoolie. On her blog, Tiny House Foodie, Carmen demonstrates how cooking can still be a joy in a small space. Says she, "Our family jokes that we live in the space of a 'sardine tin,' but we eat like kings."

Website:
https://tinyhousefoodie.com/

Facebook:
https://www.facebook.com/TinyHouseFoodie/

Instagram:
https://www.instagram.com/carmenroseshenk/

Twitter:
https://twitter.com/CarmenShenk

YouTube:
https://www.youtube.com/channel/UCMUpyM_x-WXF-9dwxZSGyblg

Xaver Wilhelmy - Certified Pipe Organ Builder:
http://www.geshenke.com/

Fueled by Essential Oils:
https://anoint-ed.com/
Young Living Wholesale Membership #12282510